THE BLENDED CHURCH:

THE EMERGENCE OF
MULTICULTURAL CHRISTIANITY

By Dehner Maurer

ED

I pray these words give
Life as you read. May God
Raise you up + use you
For His Glory
Because Of Colum

DM

The Blended Church
ISBN: 978-0-88144-164-2
Copyright © 2010 by Dehner Maurer

Published by
Thorncrown Publishing
9731 East 54th Street
Tulsa, OK 74146
www.yorkshirepublishing.com

ENDORSEMENT

We must understand the cultural divide between the races in a hurting and segregated society. Tastefully written and sensitive to the needs of the divided world, this insightful and inspirational book will be used to set the captives free. Dr. Dehner's experiences as pastor of The Blended Church will encourage you to be more effective for the Kingdom. A required reading for all missionaries and pastors who minister in today's hurting world.

Dr. Hin Hiong Khoo
Founder
International Christian Mission

DEDICATION:

To Kimmy for twenty five years of marriage, I love you!
My children Kristal and John along with
my parents Dick and Sarah.
Thanks Blended church, staff and elders
for believing in the dream.
I must also mention GP's new love, Shalom.

TABLE OF CONTENTS

FOREWORD

Martin Luther King, Jr. expressed his dream "that one day on the red hills of Georgia, the sons of former slaves and the sons of former slave owners will be able to sit down together at the table of brotherhood," and that his "four little children will one day live in a nation where they will not be judged by the color of their skin but by the content of their character."

Almost 50 years have passed since Dr. King spoke those words in the midst of a struggle to build bridges between races, and an honest examination will reveal that the yearning he expressed is still not fulfilled in our culture, especially in the church. Tremendous advances have been made in race relations, to the extent that America's first Black president occupies the Oval Office. Minorities have moved past the doors of schools and executive offices of corporations. The ethnic complexion of suburban neighborhoods has changed, but the congregations at a typical Sunday church service remain basically the same. In addition to identifying churches as Baptist, Methodist and otherwise, we still describe them as "white" or "black."

In a first century world characterized by bitter racial, cultural, national and social hatred, the Christian church was a model of reconciliation and harmony. Speaking of

Christ and the church, the apostle Paul wrote: "For he himself is our peace, who has made the two one and has destroyed the barrier, the dividing wall of hostility...His purpose was to create in himself one new man out of the two, thus making peace, and in this one body to reconcile both of them to God through the cross, by which he put to death their hostility" (Eph. 2:14-16 NIV).

In this book Dehner Maurer presents a thorough and revealing analysis of the church's failure to fulfill its divinely appointed purpose regarding racial harmony and prescribes practical and biblical principles to meet the problem. He shows that true reconciliation goes beyond token integration and statements of equality to a spirit of unity and purpose. Such a spirit begins in one-on-one relationships in which we view the other person as someone whom God loves dearly and for whom Christ died. Maurer enforces the principles he espouses with both biblical and contemporary illustrations, primarily from his own church situation.

People in pews and pulpits of all churches and races will profit from reading this book and implementing its teachings.

Dr. Myles Munroe

ACKNOWLEDGEMENTS:

I would like to thank Pastor David Gibson, Bertha Williams, Earline Foster, Old School (Emily), Sheila, Eliza, and Allison. With out your support, this would not have not been possible.

SECTION ONE

THE FUTURE

A NEW STRATEGIC VISION FOR THE CHURCH

There's a new move of God that's about to sweep across the land of this great country. America is about to see a new face arise within the church. It's the explosion of the multi-cultural church—a church that looks like heaven, from every tribe, tongue, race and nation. It's the church of unified nations in Christ. It has been prophesied about, dreamed of, preached on, and is now arising. This county has a bad track record concerning racism and its treatment of people who looked different. The church started to rise in the days of the civil rights, but then slacked up before the job was finished. However, the time is at hand for Matthew 28 to come alive like never before. This great commission we all know, understand, and want to fulfill has now progressed to another level. We can see and feel the heart of Jesus in this passage, the one who became sin that we may stand before the Father blameless.

MATTHEW 28:18-20

And Jesus came and spoke to them, saying, "All authority has been given to Me in heaven and on earth. Go therefore and make disciples of all the nations, baptizing them in the name of the Father and of the Son and of the Holy Spirit, teaching them to observe all things that I have commanded you; and lo, I am with you always, even to the end of the age." Amen

A church should consist of people from every nation and ethnic group. There was a time when we trained believers and sent them across the oceans and to remote islands. This has been very effective for the cause of Christ. Heroes have risen to the top, suffered great persecution, and we have seen the fruit of their labor. The good news of Jesus has spread throughout the world. However, times have changed.

The world has grown smaller due to our advancement of travel. Communication worldwide is open to all, and business trade routes have significantly changed our opportunities. Globalization in the 21st century has shifted geographical and cultural boundaries, and the nations are now at our door step. I've traveled to India, Myanmar, Indonesia, Malaysia, Singapore, and many other countries to preach the gospel. Today all of these nations are within my own city. Christ has now brought them to us. Jesus said to reach all nations and now has them living in our neighborhoods.

Recently, I had been praying for the church in Pakistan. A few days later I was riding my bike through my neighborhood with my little Chihuahua named Brown. I heard him bark and dash across the street towards someone. It was then I noticed a man dressed in his Black Shalwar Kameez. This is traditional Pakistani men's clothing. Wow, what an opportunity that was standing right in front of me, and yes, I have already started to build a relationship with him.

There has been much talking about the open borders among the political groups and media today. While I don't have the answers for this situation, and would not dare go there in this book (smile), I do see the Lord giving the church new doors to walk through to reach nations. David Boyd shares, "Matthew 28:19 is telling us to go culturally, not geographically. God intends everyone to move out of his or her ethnic group. If we really wanted to obey the Great Commission, we would build multicultural churches in which cross-cultural communication would happen naturally. The local church must take ownership to reach all ethnic groups within its sphere of influence. The Church must effectively include people of diverse ethnic backgrounds."[1] We are to reach out to all nations, to all cultures, and no people group can be isolated or forgotten.

Boyd further comments on Matthew 28 by bringing out a point that will advance the church into another strategic vision if we could just dare to listen. He says, "What makes the great commission so amazing is Jesus said to these mono-culture Hebraic Jews, who would have nothing to do with anyone who was not Jewish, that they should go out and make disciples of other ethnic people. Missions should primarily be a function of the local church, not mission structures. If Churches were multicultural, we could cross cultural barriers, and bicultural people could then be prepared to take the Gospel back to their ethnic groups in their homeland."[2]

George Yancey, a leading researcher for breaking racial barriers, says, "It is common for the American church to make a tremendous effort to support foreign mission work in order to reach people of different races in other countries and yet do little, if anything, about reaching people of different races in their own cities."[3] I pray that this quote will stretch us and cause us to move out of our comfort zones. We should consider the fruit and great harvest of integrating and planting multicultural churches and the consequences if we don't.

We must charge ahead with the commission to bring all nations to Christ. As Christians with the wisdom of the Holy Spirit we should lead the world with a fresh vision and not lag behind with yesterday's ideas. A great illustration is the sale of the coffee bean. For years coffee was the main drink for family and friends to sit and communicate together. When I was growing up the adults sat around drinking coffee. It was young people who decided coffee was boring and chose Coke instead. In the years following, coffee began to see a huge fall in sales, while Coke, Pepsi and the like, stormed into the future. It was years later when someone decided to sell the same coffee bean just in a different package. They actually had the audacity to put ice and chocolate in the coffee.

As a church we can preach the same Jesus, just in a relevant way, or in a different package. The commission has not changed, the way we fulfill it has. We are the peacemakers; we are the voice of Jesus on this earth. For our voice to be heard we must represent each culture. We should be the coat of many colors to a hurting world. There is an anointing to build multicultural churches today.

I live in a city with a large college campus. One day, after starting this book, I was driving by the campus and noticed the different cultures that were exhibited. This reminded me of a college ministry that no longer exists. This ministry focused on reaching different cultures on the campus and then sending the people back to their countries as missionaries and church planters. Have we lost focus on the call? Have we lacked the strategy? International students were the first signs of the coming movement. "In 1945, there were some 15,000 foreign students attending American colleges and universities. Today there are more than 550,000 enrolled, and up to a million in the US on student visas. Just think what would happen if the half a million foreign students now in the United States heard the gospel and accepted its truth! Imagine the impact these students could make if they allowed themselves to be trained here in the states as full-time ministers of the gospel, and then returned to their own international countries as dedicated Christian missionaries and world leaders."[4]

A church with multicultural blends that represents many nations draws positive attention from the world. The world is used to seeing the church divided but one that stands in unity has a powerful voice. When they see us loving people without prejudice, they will then give us a chance to speak. This is our avenue to greater influence in the world. "Then they will know," Jesus said.

The Prayer of Jesus for Unity in John 17

In John chapter 17, we see and hear Jesus praying. Technically, we should probably call *this* the Lord's Prayer. This prayer can be broken down in three sections. In the first section Jesus is praying for himself, in the second section he is praying for his disciples, and in the third section he is praying for us. Starting at verse 20 Jesus says, *"I do not pray for these alone, but also for those who will believe in me through their word; that they all may be one, as you, father, are in me, and I in you; that they also may be one in us, that the world may believe that you sent me."*

Could it be that people do not realize the Father has sent the Son because the church is not one? Until we come to the unity of faith, don't expect to see revival. One of the major issues of unity is racism in the church. If the church can't worship as one, don't expect the world to come knocking at our doors. The church is the answer and has the answer it is summed up in the prayer Jesus prayed in John 17. "Then, the world will know," He said. We have to unify to have a voice. As soon as my church began to break down the walls of racism, the city took notice and came to us. What they had attempted to do for years with limited success, we were doing in little time with great success.

The church should be the model of unity and answer to racism in our cities. Racism is sin, and the church left a sin issue to the government to fix. The church alone can fix the sin issues in our communities. The tragedy occurs when Christians then complain at the city for taking steps to fight against racism such as busing, affirmative action, and the like. We can't blame the government for the church's lack of action. The power of unity has been studied and talked about within the walls of the church for years without any change.

Cultures from all over the world are entering our own back yard, and we have done little to make them feel at home in our local churches. Have we done all we can do to make them guests and not isolated them? Have we tried to Americanize them instead of reaching them with the good news? We do not need to take away their cultural identity to bring them to Christ. It's the multicultural church that can celebrate their differences while bringing them into the body of Christ, and do this with great success. We need to celebrate who we are. We must celebrate in our diversity. My church is called The Blended Church. Blended does not mean conformity. Unity is not conformity, but unity celebrates its diversity. We're not trying to conform to all look the same. Thank God we all don't look alike. It's about unity and celebrating our diversity. The power is in the blending within the diversity.

One way to illustrate the blending of diversity is my favorite drink called a Mint Mocha Chip Frappuccino. I know I'm on the coffee kick again, I admit I have issues. There is no match for this blended coffee. Here is Starbuck's definition: "An indulgent blend of rich Starbuck's coffee with cool mint chocolate, chocolate chips and ice, mixed with our creamy frappuccino coffee base and topped with sweet whipped cream and a mocha drizzle. The unique thin mint cookie flavor is something you never tasted in a syrup before." This thing is awesome. Every time they give me one, the first thing I look for is the big white mound of whipped cream and all the chocolate. If they don't put much chocolate on it, I say, "Put some more chocolate syrup on that thing please." Without the white it's no good. Without the black, it's different. Without the mixtures, it's not the stand-out. When you blend them together in unity then it is something to celebrate. Every time I drink it, I pull the straw all the way out, and put it back. I get a little chocolate, a little whipped cream, and a bit of mint all in one sip. When I get to the end of the drink, you can hear "sccchhh." There is power in a blended diversity that is rooted in unity.

No longer can we use comments like, "I'm color-blind." In all honesty it even further denies the real issues of racism. To say we are color-blind is to say let's forget who God made us. It would be suggesting that God really made a mistake.

We all see in color, and that is the way God made us. If you did not see colors then you would be going to an ophthalmologist and pursuing any other kind of help you could find. To be color-blind would mean that your eyes are not working properly. So why would we say we're color-blind? Do we think it is politically correct to say we're color-blind? Maybe it allows us to side step the issue of racism?

The multicultural church is our reply for racism and the blueprint for reaching the nations. The multicultural church is the cry of the Holy Spirit for America today. I believe it's now time for the church to arise. Jesus is building His church, and she will prevail as the light. However, it can't be done while we remain divided. A house divided against itself will not stand.

MATTHEW 12:25

But Jesus knew their thoughts, and said to them: "Every kingdom divided against itself is brought to desolation, and every city or house divided against itself will not stand.

We all know the statement, "United, we stand and divided, we fall." The concept is, unless the people are united, then it is easy to destroy them. This is in direct contrast to the phrase, divide and conquer, which is a combination of military, political, and economic strategy of destroying an enemy. The principles of unity and division are based in God's word. God wants us in unity, and the devil has used our division against us. The terms unity, agreement, and one accord are compelling word studies in the New Testament. The words "one accord", in Acts 1:14, 2:1, 2:46, 4:24, 5:12, reveal their secret to the dynamic ability to affect the world.

When Jesus spoke of the concept of agreeing, the root of that word is symphonize. A symphony shows the value and beauty of individuals coming together. On their own, the music doesn't amount to much, but together the experience is unmatched. The multicultural church in harmony will allow Jesus to shine in His glory. When we come together in unity, there is no stopping us!

We are seeing more multicultural churches than ever before but the numbers remain at less than 10%. "America will not be won to Christ by establishing more churches like the vast majority of those we now have. Consequently, more and different churches are needed. Many people are falling through the cracks of existing churches. In an increasingly multicultural, urban society, there are groups of people who do not fit into the traditional categories of churches.

- ◆ Interracial couples and families
- ◆ Ethnic people who prefer speaking English
- ◆ Urban and suburban people in major metropolitan areas who appreciate living, working, and ministering in the midst of ethnic diversity"[5]

Churches that reflect nations are a new sphere of God's Spirit moving across our lands that simultaneously accomplish the great commission.

CHAPTER TWO

THE CHANGING FACE OF AMERICA

The new majority in America will be people of color,[6] yet the church has remained engrafted in its segregation of a white church/black church. It's the elephant in the church sanctuary. Racism has stained our message. There seems to be no real unity, only tolerance and acceptance. The church is the only answer for the sin of racism in our cities, but how can we fight against it if we continue to worship segregated? If we don't move ahead we will never have the influence we were meant to have. What's worse is we will stifle His voice.

The U.S. is a "browning nation, which is shifting rapidly toward being a polyglot of brown, yellow, black, white and mestizo (mixed). For example, California's population is now predominately "minority"—Hispanics, African Americans, Asians and 'mixed' groups now comprise 50% of the state's population. This will be a reality in Arizona by 2005, in Texas by 2010, and for the entire nation by the year 2050. The last Census for the first time gave people the opportunity to choose more than one race to describe themselves, and 2.4% of the country's 281.4 million citizens did so. Multiracial or mixed-race Americans currently number at least 6.8 million. As this 'blending of America' continues, racial lines may blur until the 'melting pot' becomes a harmonious 'we-are-the-world' reality. By 2050, 21% of Americans will be claiming mixed ancestry, according to some projections."[7]

The "Asian population is projected to triple, from 11 million to 33 million. This will slightly more than double their population share, from 4 percent to 8 percent. According to the projections, the non-Hispanic white and black populations would increase more slowly than other groups. Non-Hispanic whites are expected to increase from 196 million in 2000 to 210 million in 2050, representing a 7 percent increase. Beginning in the 2040s, non-Hispanic whites are projected to start losing population and to make up 50 percent of the total population in 2050, a drop from 69 percent in 2000. The black population is projected to grow from 36 million to 61 million in 2050, an increase of 71 percent. That change will increase blacks' share of the nation's population from 13 percent in 2000 to 15 percent in 2050."[8]

The truth is that the world has moved in around us, and our world as we know it is changing. We can no longer hide in our little ethnic cocoons and pretend that it is all about us. Globally, "almost 200 million people live in a country that is different from their place of birth. Thirteen and a half million are refugees. Within this worldwide wave of migration, the United States is home to the largest population of international migrants. Thirty –three million people –about twelve percent of the U.S. population –are foreign born."[9] These statistics are staggering and only growing. America has a changing face. It looks different than when we grew up. Just from the statistics alone it shows the church will also have to look different. The Census Bureau noted that minorities currently represent nearly half of the children being born in the U.S. and that this year could be a "tipping point" during which the number of babies born to minorities outnumbers those born to whites. Connect that fact with the combination of all "minorities" are expected to become the majority of our nation's population within the next years, and we have an enormous challenge.

Is the church in front or behind this coming curve? Does the church represent or reflect this change, or are we stuck in the past? If the church refuses to change, we will be viewed as irrelevant to the world, or we will be viewed as a small group of people in the corner that's living with blinders on. In his research, Charles Foster says, "Even though fifty years after the beginning of the civil rights movement have passed most congregations continue to be among the most racially segregated institutions in the US society."[10] Tony Campolo, who I would consider a pioneer leader against racism in the church, states that "Christianity has been deeply compromised by its participation in a culture of racism. Indeed cultural and racial homogeneity would seem to be a dominant characteristic of congregations in the United States and Canada."[11] Our dominate characteristic is cultural and racial homogeneity—that HURTS! Jesus said it should be love.

JOHN 13:34-35

A new commandment I give to you, that you love one another; as I have loved you, that you also love one another. By this all will know that you are My disciples, if you have love for one another."

We need a multicultural church in this nation to rise to the forefront as a response of the Holy Spirit to the racial wars that exist in America. Most everyone in the United States, whether or not they go to church, can tell you the church contributes to the racism problem in America. I understand I'm passionate about this subject, but what amazes me is how we (the church) are not. The view of our segregation in America and the American church from the world's perspective is tragic. Elaine Sciolino, author of *Persian Mirrors: The Elusive Face of Iran,* says, "Just as race is the great problem for American democracy, gender is the fault line of the Islamic world."

This author points out that race is a great problem for our American society; it is comparative to the issue of the segregation of women in the Islamic world. If even people from Iran can see it, why have we been so blind? It's amazing that the world watches us and knows it, other religions watch us live racism out, and we're the only ones who won't acknowledge it. Most churches claim to be open to all, but the fact is we preach segregation and demonstrate it by our division every Sunday morning.

I pray you will not be upset at some of the tough comments and quotes that are used in this book. In no way is this book meant to attack the church. I know Jesus is building His church and the gates of hell will not prevail (Matthew 16:18). I love the church and have given my life to help it grow. This book has one purpose: to challenge what we have accepted as normal. We must change in order to grow and bring about a new wave of lives being brought into the kingdom.

It was at a conference that a speaker made a statement that upset me. After a couple of days of his statement rolling around in me, I began to realize that sometimes we have to be deeply offended or be critically challenged to be motivated to change. Some quotes in this book may seem to be offensive, may hurt, or anger some, but this subject can't be watered down or be non-offensive. Racism seems to be a subject discussed too many times with no action. I firmly believe we could all grow in this area. We can all do more.

James Cone (I don't agree with his stance on black liberation theology) asks a question we should all deeply consider. "Could it be true that racism lives because we do nothing, and when we don't do something we are racist?"[12] Let me recapitulate my purpose of that quote. I do not think Christians are emphatically or deliberately practicing racism. Could it be we're not sure how to take the next step, thinking we have done enough, or that by ignoring the subject we have overcome or will overcome racism? We will tackle these questions later in more detail.

The Great Adventure

This book is about an adventure of challenging the status quo of the church's stance or lack of one on racism. It is about the good, the bad, and the ugly of doing something different for the Kingdom. It's about the struggles we have faced at church, and then the glorious experience of seeing blacks and whites come together. From there we have seen 30 nations of people come worship as a family, in unity for Jesus every Sunday morning. I have felt the pain and been wounded by the struggles of fighting racism in our church.

I am reminded of those who loved us and even wanted us to succeed but said it couldn't be done. Yes, that even included many pastors and leaders in our communities. We received phone calls from other churches telling us we were embarrassing the churches in the city. Racism stirs things up in people that are unimaginable. I will never forget the time in our earlier days that we had begun to share the message on racism in the church.

We produced a show on public access television in Indianapolis. After sharing a message of "a church that looked like heaven," we were greeted by a great surprise. I pulled up to the building and attempted to unlock the front door. To my astonishment, the key would not fit into the lock, and while not realizing what had happened, I went to the back door with the same result. It was then I began to stare into the lock realizing they had been super glued. I will never forget the emotion of anger, bewilderment, and awe that a person would attack a church.

Since those days, I've come to realize that racism can live deep within individuals and the anger and hatred it brings out are inconceivable, even among Christians. One night our windows were blown out by bottle rockets with racial slurs painted all over our church walls. So many times I have been called a traitor, a sellout, a n***** lover. The church has been talked about and even churches have been bold about their stance against us. Some have said we were embarrassing to Christ and our "new doctrine" of "blending the races" is blasphemy.

Friedrich Otto Hertz once said, "At the heart of racism is the religious assertion that God made a creative mistake when He brought some people into being."[13] There has been a lot of pain caused by being talked about by Christians and watching them walk out of service when they saw someone who was a different color than they were. I have heard comments like: "We should worship with our own kind" or "I'm not racist, but..." Misconceptions live in each of us without us even realizing it. The white Christians are saying, "I'm not racist," or "I have a black friend." Black Christians are saying, "All whites are racist."

Along with the pain, I've also experienced the sweet, refreshing presence of the Lord, which comes when people from all tribes, tongues, and races worship together. It brings momentum to a church. Growth occurs and an indescribable experience takes place that even the unsaved can feel. We have had unbelievers come visit us on Sunday services and return the next week just because the awe of 30 nations meeting together. Many times they end up giving their hearts to Christ.

The purpose of this book is to challenge you, your church, your connection groups, and your circle of friends to begin the process of integrating. The thoughts that you can't and the worries of how will be dissolved by reading this book. Through 15 years of research, planting a thriving multicultural church, and helping others do it, I have the answers to your questions and the steps to help you begin. So let's get started!

CHAPTER THREE

THE MULTICULTURAL CHURCH IN SCRIPTURE.

The multicultural church played an instrumental part of expanding the gospel in the book of Acts. I believe the latter will be greater than the former so what lies ahead will be inconceivable. Many have failed to realize, or just overlooked all the scripture says about the multicultural church. It is easy to read the scripture to confirm what we already believe. Let's take a new look and see some fresh revelation in this exciting journey.

ACTS 17:26

"And then He made from one blood every nation..."

"All mankind was one in origin, all created by God and all descended from one common ancestor. This removed all imagined justification for the belief that Greeks were innately superior to barbarians, as it removes all imagined justification for parallel police today. Neither in nature, nor in the old creation, nor in the new is there any room for any ideas of racial superiority."[14] Guess what the word nation is? Ethnos, Ethnicity—from every nation: one blood. And then He made from one blood every ethnicity. That means the same blood is in us all, and we're all related, and from the one man and one true God. How is it, we look down on one another just because we look different from each other?

GALATIANS 3:28

"There's neither Jew nor Greek, neither slave nor free, there's neither male nor female, for you are all one in Christ Jesus."

Something radically new and different has occurred within this baptized community so that "there is neither Jew nor Greek, slave nor free, male nor female." In some sense, these fundamental human distinctions have been altered or superseded by the new relationship of being "in Christ." This is beyond dispute.[15] This is what the New Testament says. There is neither Jew nor Greek. God had only two people groups. It was either the Jew or the Gentile. That was the racial divide, if there was ever a racial divide.

God eventually broke that down and said He didn't care if we were Jew, Greek, or Gentile. He said "come in," we're all welcome. That means the same redemption. It doesn't matter if you are black or white. We have the same redemption by the same blood of Jesus Christ, who died for us. Gentile, Greek, German, Jew, Hindi, Asian, it doesn't matter. The Bible gives us no ground for saying that one race is superior or inferior to any other race. We celebrate who we are, but we come together in unity, and we share the message of Christ.

In God's holy sight, all men are indeed equal; "all have sinned, and fall short of the glory of God" (Rom. 3:23; cf. 2:11; 3:9–18; 5:12, 18). Furthermore, "the same Lord is Lord of all, and is rich to all that call on him" (Rom. 10:12). For a Jew to confess himself to be a Christian, and then to refuse to eat with Christians from the Gentiles, or to regard himself as being in any way superior to them in moral worth, is an abomination to the Lord. Similarly today the church cannot tolerate hurtful distinctions. All believers are in a sense one person, one body "in Christ" (I Cor. 10:17; 12:12; Col. 3:15), for he who is the Son of David is also the Son of man; he who is "the seed of Abraham" is in addition "the seed of the woman." From God's side the Holy Spirit, and from man's side Spirit-imparted faith, link believers with Christ, and thereby with one another.[16]

In the following pages, we will share many passages from the book of Acts. Dr. A. Charles Ware shares in his book *Prejudice and the People of God* that "the multicultural and multiethnic nature of the church revealed in the book of Acts is obvious."[17] Take a close look. The diversity in the backgrounds of the leaders of the church at Antioch shows the cosmopolitan nature of the church.[18]

ACTS 13:1–3

Now in the church that was at Antioch there were certain prophets and teachers: Barnabas, Simeon who was called Niger, Lucius of Cyrene, Manaen who had been brought up with Herod, the Tetrarch, and Saul. As they ministered to the Lord and fasted, the Holy Spirit said, "Now separate to Me Barnabas and Saul for the work to which I have called them." Then, having fasted and prayed, and laid hands on them, they sent them away.

This is the church God anointed, and it was multicultural in staff, leadership, and congregation. The Bible tells us that Barnabas was a Levite, and he was from Cyprus.

Simeon had the nickname Niger that came from a Latin word. The Latin word means this: he had dark skin. The name Simeon, however, is a Jewish name. Some people believe this is the same man who carried the cross of Jesus.[19] The next man was Lucius of Cyrene. Cyrene is the northern part of Africa. So we already have a multicultural mix. And then we have Manaen, who had been brought up with Herod the Tetrarch. This guy has a Gentile name, but he hung out with Herod. He was a friend of Herod. He was part of the palace of Herod. He may have worked for Herod. Then we have Saul. We know he was a Jew, yet he had Roman citizenship.

We see a multicultural mix within the structure of the leadership of the church. All the missionaries who were ever sent out were sent out from Antioch. The elders wouldn't send them out from Jerusalem so God had to send persecution to kick them out. They were so worried about what they were going to eat, what they were going to wear, or their circumcision that they missed the heart of the gospel. We've done the same thing at church. We say that this is the way we've always done it. It doesn't matter how you've always done it; what does the Bible say you should be doing?

ACTS 11:26

And when he had found him, he brought him to Antioch. So it was that for a whole year they assembled with the church and taught a great many people. And the disciples were first called Christians in Antioch.

The disciples were called Christians first in Antioch. Since the outpouring of the Holy Spirit on the day of Pentecost in Jerusalem, the followers of Jesus referred to themselves as brothers, disciples, believers, saints, and those who belonged to the Way. The time had come to adopt a definitive and descriptive name for the people who accepted Jesus as their Lord and Savior. The name *Christians* was used first in Antioch in the multicultural setting of that city.[20] They made such an impact that the world began to say that they were like Christ. They didn't say that about the church in Jerusalem. Remember when Jesus said, "May they be one so the world may know that You have sent Me?" Now we know why we see the power of God in Antioch.

ACTS 11:27

And in these days prophets came from Jerusalem to Antioch.

The power of God was in Antioch. That's where people were being touched and changed. The presence of God rested here, I believe, because of two things. The first is because they were a church that looked like heaven in unity and second because they were a sending church. The Jerusalem church died out because they ignored these two issues. I know that's a strong statement but really meditate on it.

MARK 11:17

Then He taught, saying to them, "Is it not written, 'My house shall be called a house of prayer for all nations?[21]

Why don't we quote the second part, *for all nations,* all ethnicity? That's the word, "ethnos" which means all groups of people. That's when we come in and pray in power. It's when all groups come together, and we are in unity and one accord. I always hear the first part of the scripture quoted, but it must be used in context.

We know this as The Great Commission:

MATTHEW 28:16-20

Then the eleven disciples went away into Galilee, to the mountain which Jesus had appointed for them. When they saw Him, they worshiped Him; but some doubted.

And Jesus came and spoke to them, saying, "All authority has been given to Me in heaven and on earth. Go therefore and make disciples of all the nations, baptizing them in the name of the Father and of the Son and of the Holy Spirit, teaching them to observe all things that I have commanded you, and lo, I am with you always, even to the end of the age." Amen.

Jesus said to go to all ethnic groups of people. As we discussed earlier, all nations are clearly now within our walls. The harvest fields are now ready to be reached for Christ. In John 4 when Jesus preached this, he said, *'Behold the fields are ripe for the harvest"*.

After his statement they all looked up, and here came the harvest, a group of multicultural people. Some people may think I'm taking racism to the extreme but the people we are not reaching, letting slide through the gaps, and the future is the different ethnic groups. We have overlooked the details of this great truth Jesus tried to share. Let me share a contrasting definition that brings to light the present situation we are battling. Prejudice is to racism what lust is to adultery. Racism is this: having hatred toward another group. Prejudice is this: having suspicion or judgment upon another group without understanding all the facts. We need to change our mindset that devalues those that are different than us. You and I are called to reach them ALL.

Let's look at another biblical story. God has scattered the Jerusalem church, and they are out doing ministry. We know that Phillip is preaching, and in Acts 9, Peter raises the dead. Think about that, Peter raises a dead lady. Peter speaks to her, tells her to rise, and she comes to life. Peter is having a revival and you know he is excited. Let's be real; Peter's on fire and walking on a cloud seeing all that is happening. He's witnessing and sharing the story with everybody. In the midst of the revival he is seeing, I believe God wants him to reach a new level of maturity, so he can experience even more. So let's look at this teaching moment.

ACTS 10:1-8

There was a certain man in Caesarea called Cornelius, a centurion of what was called the Italian Regiment, ²a devout man and one who feared God with all his household, who gave alms generously to the people, and prayed to God always.

³About the ninth hour of the day he saw clearly in a vision an angel of God coming in and saying to him, "Cornelius!" ⁴And when he observed him, he was afraid, and said, "What is it, Lord?" So he said to him, "Your prayers and your alms have come up for a memorial before God. ⁵Now send men to Joppa, and send for Simon whose surname is Peter. ⁶He is lodging with Simon, a tanner, whose house is by the sea. He will tell you what you must do." ⁷And when the angel who spoke to him had departed, Cornelius called two of his household servants and a devout soldier from among those who waited on him continually. ⁸So when he had explained all these things to them, he sent them to Joppa.

God already knew what He was going to do in Peter. His plans involved talking to Cornelius the day before. God is not surprised at what you face tomorrow. If you walk into work, and you are demoted, God already knew. If they dissolve your job or change your position, God already knew, and He has a plan. He knows when you get home and your child doesn't act or respond the way you want him or her to. He knows when situations don't work the way you want them to. He knows a bill that is coming that you don't know about. He knows it all, and He has a plan for all of it.

Back at Joppa, God was preparing Peter for an encounter that would change his life. This lesson is about racism. It showed Peter how he must change his opinion on different cultures while the men sent by Cornelius were on their way. "Peter is a Jew, who since childhood has learned not to enter the home of a Gentile and not to break bread with a non-Jew. He must now learn to overcome his prejudice and accept God-fearing Gentiles, who believe in Jesus, as brothers and sisters. Through a vision, God prepares Peter for the meeting with Cornelius and his household."[22]

I don't know if you've ever prayed on the roof of your house or while looking up to the sky, but it is one of the most powerful ways you can ever pray. Many times when we do go to pray, and we're so loud and so talkative that we never give God room to speak to our hearts. So God is going to come in and mess up Peter's prayer. God doesn't want to hear a lot from Peter, He wants to talk to Peter. The problem is like us, Peter has his own agenda. He's on a mountain of excitement from all that has happened. He was just used of God to raise someone from the dead.

God has a burning bush experience for Peter. So Peter gets hungry and falls into a trance. God presents food to Peter that is against everything he has ever been taught. According to Leviticus Chapter 11,[23] these are things he cannot eat. I imagine there's lobster on that sheet and a big, 'ol pig with some ribs, bacon, and brisket. They smell good and look good, but they are things that he wouldn't even think about touching.

ACTS 10:13-16

[13]*And a voice came to him, "Rise, Peter, kill and eat."* [14]*But Peter said, "Not, so, Lord! For I have never eaten anything common or unclean." * [15]*And a voice spoke to him again the second time, "what God has cleansed you must not call common."*

[16]*This was done three times. And the object was taken up into heaven again.*

Peter tells God that he won't eat it because that's not the way it's done in the Jewish culture. He knew it was God telling him to eat because he called him Lord, but he still told Him no. This is like saying, "We love You, God, and we want to praise You and worship You, but that's not the way we do it around here. This is the way we like to worship God. We don't want people of different cultures in here."

ACTS 10:15

[15]*And a voice spoke to him again the second time, "what God has cleansed you must not call common."*

¹⁶This was done three times. And the object was taken up into heaven again.

God had to tell Peter to eat three times, and Peter said no each time. Here is a mighty man of God, but still his culture is keeping him from what God has given him. His culture is keeping him from moving into the new place God has for him. His culture is keeping him from reaching people who Christ wants him to reach. His parents and his parents' parents taught him that eating this food was wrong.

You've got to be aware of what culture tries to say and what Christ is saying. Some of the things you have learned because of culture you need to get rid of. Don't make God come three times speaking to you, and you keep telling him no. The lesson God teaches Peter in this vision of the clean and unclean animals is that God has removed the barriers he once erected to separate his people from the surrounding nations. The barrier between the Jewish Christian and the Samaritan Christian had been removed when Peter and John went to Samaria to accept the Samaritan believers as full members of the church. Now the time has come to extend the same privilege to Gentile believers.

God, not man, removes the barrier that separates the Jew from the Gentile. God instructs Peter to accept Gentile believers in the Christian church. God, not Peter, opens the gates of heaven to the Gentiles. God himself inaugurates a new phase of a gospel ministry for Peter. Before Jesus ascended to heaven, he told the apostles to make disciples of all nations by baptizing and teaching believers regardless of race and color (Matt. 28:19–20).[24] They knew what Jesus had said, but they struggled with His words that went against their culture. The church has been separated by racism for years but that does not make it right. From here God leads Peter to Cornelius' house, and he hears the story of the vision of Cornelius.

ACTS 10:34-35

[34]*Then Peter opened his mouth and said: "In truth I perceive that God shows no partiality.* [35]*But in every nation whoever fears Him and works righteousness is accepted by Him.*

I now understand;[25] God shows no partiality. Finally, it sinks in, every tribe, race, nation, and tongue are God's. Peter now made clear his understanding of the vision. God does not show favoritism. The word favoritism literally speaks of an "acceptor of faces", and was used by Peter to refer to a God, who did not show preference among nationalities. The particular context of this statement was the Jewish prejudice against Gentiles. God does not show favoritism among nations, though he does favor those "who fear him and do what is right."[26]

GALATIANS 2:11-16

[11]*Now when Peter had come to Antioch, I withstood him to his face, because he was to be blamed;* [12]*for before certain men came from James, he would eat with the Gentiles; but when they came, he withdrew*

and separated himself, fearing those who were of the circumcision. ¹³And the rest of the Jews also played the hypocrite with him, so that even Barnabas was carried away with their hypocrisy. ¹⁴But when I saw that they were not straightforward about the truth of the gospel, I said to Peter before them all, "If you, being a Jew, live in the manner of Gentiles and not as the Jews, why do you compel Gentiles to live as Jews? ¹⁵We who are Jews by nature, and not sinners of the Gentiles, ¹⁶knowing that a man is not justified by the works of the law but by faith in Jesus Christ, even we have believed in Christ Jesus, that we might be justified by faith in Christ and not by the works of the law; for by the works of the law no flesh shall be justified.

In Galatians 2, Peter is eating and hanging out with the Gentiles. Then suddenly here came his Jewish buddies, "his homeboys." They say, "Peter, what are you doing and what are you eating? You know you can't do that. Our Law, our fathers, our culture told us we couldn't eat that." The Bible says that Peter backed off because he was worried about what somebody else thought.

Racism will take a good man and make him bad. So Peter backed off—even Barnabas, the encourager, backed off. When we read Acts, we see Barnabas is the one giving all his things away, helping the elderly people, the one encouraging, and preaching. He's the one running around pumping everyone up. He's the one telling Paul that he can do it and

Titus that he can make it. When Paul and Timothy got in a fight, Barnabas went and helped poor young Timothy.[27]

They would have gotten away with it, but Paul walked in the door. What most amazes me is that Paul walked up to Peter in front of everybody there and rebuked the leader. He didn't hide it. He said, "Peter, what is this you are doing? You found freedom in the gospel, yet…" I want this to sink in! Peter knew he had the freedom from the vision in Acts 10, but cultural pressure caused him to compromise.

So we must ask ourselves if we compromise in areas of cultural pressure. Would we do more to fight racism if we knew there would be no consequences? John McArthur makes a strong comment about this passage in Acts by saying: "A brief account of the darkest of days in the history of the gospel. By withdrawing from the Gentile believers to fellowship with the Judaizers, who held a position he knew was wrong, Peter had in appearance supported their doctrine and nullified Paul's divine teaching, especially the doctrine of salvation by grace alone through faith alone."[28] While I agree this was a dark and embarrassing moment for the church, I argue we continue to live in racism.

The white church, black church doesn't even talk now. Maybe a joint service here and there but then we leave to remain separated. We see a lot of lip service but where does that get us? We have so much more knowledge of the freedom we have in Christ now than they did, yet we're no better. We have the completed scripture in leather with multiple translations, concordances, and computer bible programs, but we are no better. What Paul accomplished in his preaching uniting the Jew and Gentile, Peter and we (Yes, I said we) have attempted to divide by our actions.

I must share Warren Wiersbe's Be Series comment on this passage. "The first thing to note is *Peter's freedom* then. He enjoyed fellowship with *all* the believers, Jews and Gentiles alike. To 'eat with the Gentiles' meant to accept them, to put Jews and Gentiles on the same level as one family in Christ. Growing up as an orthodox Jew, Peter had a difficult time learning this lesson. Jesus had taught it while He was with Peter before the Crucifixion (Matt. 15:1–20). The Holy Spirit had reemphasized it when He sent Peter to the home of Cornelius, the Roman centurion (Acts 10).

Furthermore, the truth had been accepted and approved by the conference of leaders at Jerusalem (Acts 15). Peter had been one of the key witnesses at that time. Before we criticize Peter, perhaps we should examine our own lives to see how many familiar Bible doctrines *we* are actually obeying. As we examine church history, we see that, even with a complete Bible, believers through the years have been slow to believe and practice the truths of the Christian faith. When we think of the persecution and discrimination that have been practiced in the name of Christ, it embarrasses us. It is one thing for us to defend a doctrine in a church meeting, and quite something else to put it into practice in everyday life.

Peter's freedom was threatened by *Peter's fear.* While he was in Antioch, the church was visited by some of the associates of James. (You will remember James was a strict Jew even though he was a Christian believer.) Paul does not suggest that James sent these men to investigate Peter, or even that they were officials of the Jerusalem church. No doubt they belonged to the 'circumcision party' (Acts 15:1, 5) and wanted to lead the Antioch church into religious legalism.

After his experience with Cornelius, Peter had been 'called on the carpet' and had ably defended himself (Acts 11.) But now, he became afraid. Peter had not been afraid to obey the Spirit when He sent him to Cornelius, nor was he afraid to give his witness at the Jerusalem Conference. However, with the arrival of some members of 'the opposition,' Peter lost his courage. 'The fear of man bringeth a snare' (Prov. 29:25.)

Suppose Peter and Barnabas had won that day and led the church into legalism? What might the results have been? Would Antioch have continued to be the great missionary church that sent out Paul and Barnabas? (Acts 13)"[29]

GALATIANS 2:20

I have been crucified with Christ; it is no longer I who live, but Christ lives in me; and the life which I now live in the flesh I live by faith in the Son of God, who loved me and gave Himself for me.

Do you understand that the whole context of this scripture is based on the issue of racism that Paul has just preached to Peter? There is no scripture here without preaching on racism. Paul just dealt with Peter about the racism in his heart. He's saying that he's been crucified with Christ. His culture no longer controls him. We have all died to who we were, and we are now one in Him. Racism is not an issue that can be left untouched even according to the Word! We hear this passage preached from every denomination weekly, but I have rarely heard it discussed in context with racism as the subject.

1 CORINTHIANS 15:39

"All flesh is not the same flesh but there is one kind of flesh of men..."

How many kinds of flesh of men are there? One, we all have the same skin. Skin color is "determined by the amount of melanin produced, and the proportions and distribution of its two components. This situation is true not only for skin color, but also whatever feature we may look at for no people group has anything that is, in its essence, uniquely different from that possessed by another."[30]

ROMANS 10:12

For there is no distinction between Jew and Greek, for the same Lord over all is rich to all who call upon Him.

Paul again is trying to instill that Jesus is Lord over all nations. He does not look at one group of people as being superior to another. Salvation is for all who will call on His name. For Christians to be racist is a clear dichotomy of terms. The College Press Commentary speaks on this verse saying, "For there is no difference between Jew and Gentile ... where the true Israel is concerned.

Paul has already declared, in 3:22b, that 'there is no difference' between these groups. In that verse, his point was that there is no difference between them with regard to sin, 'for all have sinned and fall short of the glory of God' (3:23); 'Jews and Gentiles alike are all under sin' (3:9). In this verse, though, the statement plays the joyful note that there is no difference between Jews and Gentiles with regard to salvation. The promise in v. 11 applies equally to all. As Peter learned through his encounter with Cornelius, 'God does not show favoritism' when it comes to salvation (Acts 10:34). The Old Covenant distinction between Jews and Gentiles was a matter of the formers' election to service; faith-righteousness as the only way of salvation is offered to all. See 1 Cor 12:13; Gal 3:28; Col 3:11."[31]

In closing this section, I would like to mention the word partiality. It's clearly mentioned all over the New Testament.

JAMES 2:9
*but if you show **partiality**, you commit sin, and are convicted by the law as transgressors.*

Also see: <u>Acts 10:34</u>, <u>Romans 2:11</u>, <u>Ephesians 6:9</u>, <u>Colossians 3:25</u>, <u>1 Timothy 5:21</u>, <u>James 2:1</u>, <u>James 2:4</u>.

The word partiality "originally meant raising someone's face or elevating the person, but it came to having the meaning of exalting someone strictly on a superficial, external basis, such as appearance, race, wealth, rank, or social status" (Lev. 19:15; Job 34:19; cf. Deut. 10:17; 15:7–10; 2 Chr. 19:7; Prov. 24:23; 28:21; Matt. 22:8–10; Acts 10:34,35; Rom. 2:11; Eph. 6:9; Col. 3:25; 4:1; 1 Pet. 1:17.)[32] K.A. Richardson says: "Can favoritism or partiality coexist with the glorious Christ of faith? Impossible."[33] Further this word is broken down: *"You show partiality."* The verb is used only here in the New Testament. It is a verbal form of the noun used in James 2:1. It means discrimination, that is "to treat people according to their outward appearance", *"You commit sin."* For James favoritism is contradictory to the command to love and is therefore, an act of sin. To *show partiality* is to *commit sin.* The verb in the phrase *"you commit sin"* makes a strong statement, literally "you are working sin," indicating that the sinning is deliberate and intentional.

It is certainly more than an error someone has fallen into, or merely some error that a person is guilty of, as the "The Everyday Version" rendering may suggest. It is, in fact, overstepping the boundary to a willful disobedience of the will of God. The person who does this is a "transgressor" as is further defined in the next clause. In certain languages, *you commit sin* will be expressed as "you have done something very wrong."[34] We as Christians need to see, love, and accept others as Christ does us. Anything less than this is unacceptable.

CHAPTER FOUR

THE MULTICULTURAL CHURCH IN HEAVEN

Have you ever thought about what the church in heaven looks like?

REVELATION 7:9-10

After these things I looked, and behold, a great multitude which no one could number, of all nations, tribes, peoples, and tongues,[35] *standing before the throne and before the Lamb, clothed with white robes, with palm branches in their hands, and crying out with a Loud voice, saying "Salvation belongs to our God who sits on the throne, and to the Lamb!"*

All ethnicity is represented; this is the church in heaven. The multitude comes "from every nation, tribe, people, and language, which speaks of the universal nature of the church. The word nation (Greek ethnos) means all the races that constitute a nation. Often several people groups make up an entire nation, so the Greek term should be understood as all-inclusive. The sequence of words nation, tribe, people, and language occurs seven times in various orders in Revelation (5:9; 7:9; 10:11; 11:9; 13:7; 14:6; 17:15).[36] Is this the church we see on earth?

We need to take a good look at the church in heaven and consider the contrast to the church we see most Sundays. How many of you can see this is not what a lot of churches look like today in America? It's not two black people among 125 white people or two white people among 125 black people. I only mention black and white here because that is the real racial divide in America. When that is dealt with, all other ethnicity groups will join in and become a part of the family. We will discuss this in detail in a later chapter.

Let's take a deeper look at REVELATION 7:9-10.

clothed with white robes[37]

That's where our unity comes; it comes in Christ. We're clothed in white because of the righteousness of Christ as we've repented of our sins. We wear the white robes of righteousness, but we celebrate our diversity. We are who we are; however, we're now new creations in Christ.[38] Being a Christian becomes greater than our culture. We still celebrate our culture; however, now we have become a part of a new breed of people.

...with palm branches in their hands[39]

Ancient Hebrew coins had palm branches on them. The palm branch represented the government. That's why they were waving the palm branches as Jesus came into Jerusalem.[40] The disciples were telling the people to put them down because the waving of branches was an action against the government saying that this one riding on the colt was coming to save them from the oppression of the Roman government.

and crying out with a loud voice, saying, "Salvation belongs to our God who sits on the throne, and to the Lamb!"

This is the church in heaven singing and rejoicing before the Lamb of God, who has taken away our sin. We also see the church in heaven and what she looks like in REVELATION 5:8-10.

Now when He had taken the scroll, the four living creatures and the twenty-four elders fell down before the Lamb, each having a harp, and golden bowls full of incense, which are the prayers of the saints. And they sang a new song, saying: "You are worthy to take the scroll, And to open its seals; For You were slain, And have redeemed us to God by Your blood. Out of every tribe and tongue and people and nation, and have made us kings and priests to our God; And we shall reign on the earth."

This is clearly a multicultural church, **out of every kindred, and tongue, and people, and nation.** The phrase "out of every tribe and language and people and nation" "occurs repeatedly in Revelation with variations in word order (7:9; 10:11; 11:9; 13:7; 14:6; 17:15). The word tribe conveys the meaning of physical ties and descent, while the term language has a much broader connotation and points to linguistic communication. The word, I have translated as people, relates to an ethnic group of common descent; and the expression nation refers to a political entity with distinct geographic boundaries. However, because of the frequent appearance of these four categories in Revelation, it is better to interpret them as an all-encompassing idiom. Jesus calls his followers, both Jews and Gentiles, from every possible place on the face of this earth, so that his people are the church universal."[41] This fourfold classification continually recurs in the Revelation. It includes all the bases of classification of mankind, all the circumstances, which separate men, the barriers which were overthrown by the redeeming work of Christ.[42]

J. Daniel Hays suggests, "That we in the church today need to ask ourselves the question as to why our earthly churches differ so much in composition from the congregations depicted in Revelation. If white churches in North America continue to maintain their ethnic exclusion of other races, particularly black Americans, are they not clearly moving in a direction that is contrary to the portrayal that John gives us? It is critical that Christians today visualize the true body of Christ and the people of God correctly. This group is not a predominantly white or black congregation. Christians together around the throne of God will rub shoulders with people of all races. How can we justify supporting and/or maintaining a system here in our local churches that works to divide and separate us?"[43]

What Color Is God's House?

Imagine a scenario where we try to decorate for God and tell him what His house should look like. When we talk of the church, we should realize it's His house, not ours. Do we want His house to look like the way we think it should because of our preconceived ideas or what we were taught? If you come to my house, I don't have a white couch, carpet, walls, refrigerator, stove, table, and everything else in my house is not white. I have a wide variety of colors. If I go to a black person's house, I guarantee that they don't have black carpet, walls, refrigerator, stove, and tables that are all black. Why is it, we think God's house should be all one color? Could it be we have not considered what God wanted?

We can look at God's creation, and see He's into diversity. Even every snowflake looks different and has its own unique identity. God wants us to be who we are; He created us each unique. We should celebrate our diversity and walk in unity. This is the key to power in the church. We have divided His church with our flawed theologies and our lackadaisical attitudes and have perpetuated the sin of racism. We must go on the offensive to combat it. We can't sit still and act like it's not happening.

We once had a young man of God leading our praise and worship services named David. He needed to catch a flight to help his brother in a church service in another city. So I took David to the airport. We arrived at the airport and there was a mess of security issues going on. Does that sound familiar? David is a humble young man and very respectful. This day he happened to be wearing a do-rag with braided hair. We only had half an hour until his plane left. People in first class kept jumping ahead of us in line, so I told David to go over to another line. David reached the service desk and began talking to a lady at the counter. He came back and said, "She won't help us, Pastor."

I said, "That's okay."

So I'm sitting there, watching and thinking, I wondered what would happen if I walked over there. So I told David to stay right there. I walked over to the same lady and told her that I needed some help. I told her that the plane would be leaving in half an hour, and that we're not making it through the line, the same things David also said to her.

"Okay," she said, "Let me see your ticket and I will get you through."

Why would she help me but not David? Is it just a coincidence or could it be racism? I'm a white man and David is a black man. Could that be the difference? Could it be because he was a young black man with a do-rag, and she thought less of him? I believe we need to challenge these things. I recently heard Billy Graham say that if he could change one thing in America, the first thing he would change is the racism that is rooted in the American church.

CHAPTER FIVE

JESUS PREACHES ON RACISM

When I ask someone, "Did you know Jesus spoke on racism?" most people will say no. This is a message that caused deep change in his disciples and those who were involved that day. I pray it will also do something deep in you. It's a message many have preached but few have heard.

JOHN 4:1- 41

Therefore, when the Lord knew that the Pharisees had heard that Jesus baptized more disciples than John (though Jesus Himself did not baptize but His disciples). He left Judea and departed again to Galilee. ⁴But He needed to go through Samaria. ⁵So He came to a city of Samaria which is called Sychar, near the plot of ground that Jacob gave his son Joseph. ⁶Now Jacob's well was there. Jesus therefore, being wearied from His journey, sat thus by the well. It was about the sixth hour. ⁷A woman of Samaria came to draw water. Jesus said to her, "Give Me a drink." ⁸For His disciples had gone away into the city to buy food. ⁹Then the woman of Samaria said to Him, "How is it that you being a Jew, ask a drink from me, a Samaritan woman?" For the Jews have no dealings with Samaritans. ¹⁰Jesus answered and said to her, "if you knew the gift of God, and who it is who says to you, 'Give Me a drink," you would have asked Him, and He would have given you living water." ¹¹The woman said to Him, "Sir, you have nothing to draw with, and the well is deep. Where then do you get that living water?" ¹²"Are you greater than our father Jacob, who gave us the well, and drank from it himself as well as his sons and his livestock?" ¹³Jesus answered and said to her, "Whoever drinks of this water will thirst again, ¹⁴"but whoever drinks of the water that I shall give him will never thirst. But the water that I shall give him will become in him a fountain of water springing up into everlasting life." ¹⁵The woman said to Him, "Sir, give me this water, that I may not thirst, nor come here to draw." ¹⁶Jesus said to her, "Go, call your husband, and come here." ¹⁷The woman answered, "I have no husband." Jesus said to her, "You have well said, ' I have no husband,' "for you have had five husbands, and the one whom you now have is not your husband, in that you spoke truly." ¹⁹The woman said to Him, "Sir, I perceive that you are a prophet." ²⁰"Our fathers worshiped on this mountain, and you Jews say that in Jerusalem is the place where one ought to worship." [21]Jesus said to her, "Woman, believe Me, the hour is coming when you will neither on this mountain, nor in Jerusalem, worship the Father." [22]You worship what you do not know; we know what we worship, for salvation is of the Jews." [23]"But the hour is coming, and now is, when the true worshipers will worship the Father in spirit and truth; for the Father is seeking such to worship Him. [24]"God is spirit, and those who worship Him must worship in spirit and truth." [25]And the woman said to Him, "I know that Messiah is coming" (who is called Christ). "When He comes, He will tell us all things." [26]Jesus said to her, "I who speak to you am He." [27]And at this point His disciples came and they marveled that He talked with a woman; yet no one said, "What do You seek?" or, "Why are You talking with her?" [28]The woman then left her water pot, went her way into the city, and said to the men, [29]"Come, see a Man who told me all things that I ever did. Could this be the Christ?" [30]Then they went out of the city and came to Him. [31]In the meantime His disciples urged him, saying, "Rabbi, eat." [32]But He said to them, "I have food to eat of which you do not know." [33]Therefore the disciples said to one another, "Has anyone brought Him anything to eat?" [34]Jesus said to them, "My food is to do the will of Him who sent me, and to finish His *work." ³⁵"Do you not say, ' There are still four months and then comes the harvest'? Behold, I say to you, lift up your eyes and look at the fields for they are already white for the harvest! ³⁶"And he who reaps receives wages, and gathers fruit for eternal life, that both he who sows and he who reaps may rejoice together." ³⁷"For in this one saying is true: 'One sows and another reaps.' ³⁸"I sent you to reap that which you have not labored; others have labored, and you have entered into their labors." ³⁹And many of the Samaritans of that city believed in Him because of the word of the woman who testified, "He told me all that I ever did." ⁴⁰So when the Samaritans had come to Him, they urged Him to stay with them; and He stayed there two days. ⁴¹And many more believed because of His own word.*

Jesus and His disciples were baptizing all these people and there was a commotion about to happen. People were upset. Why is He baptizing more people than John? However, Jesus knew that His time was not now. He knew that this wasn't the time that He needed to be promoting what He was doing. He understood there are times and seasons. We too, have to understand there are times and seasons in our lives.⁴⁴

There are times when God will promote you, and times when God wants you hidden. Times when God will give you a voice, and times when God may want you silent. Times when God may lift you up front, and times when God may want you behind. He opens doors and shuts them. You can't fight the seasons of the Lord.[45] You have got to trust God. He knows what the right timing is. He understands the seasons. So don't be hurting when you are silenced, when nobody's listening, when God is just asking you to do a small thing, and you're behind the scenes. Rejoice in that because the season will come when He says, "Move up front."

It's the principle that Jesus taught, when he said, "Don't go up to the front and try and promote yourself. Stay in the back and wait until they say to you, 'Come forward.' Then you come forward."[46] I struggled with that for years. Nothing seemed to work. I knew I had a call of God on my life, and I tried to push it and tried to promote it. It wasn't until I finally stopped, and said, "All right, I'll shut up and not say anything." That is when the time of promotion came. When I really decided to trust in the fact that He is in control and will make things work the right way, my life got easier. Let's get back to verse 3.

"And He needed to go through Samaria."[47]

Now wait a minute. Jews simply did not go through Samaria. It was culturally unacceptable, but He **needed** to. They had a little thing I like to call a city by-pass. It was very simple to go straight through, and it would have been faster. However, the Jews just went around because they didn't go to Samaria. Why didn't they go to Samaria? In 722 BC, God's judgment came upon Israel. Assyria invaded and took many of the Jewish people captives. Many of the Assyrians mistreated them and had sex with them in order to dominate them. As a consequence of this, there came about what the Jews called a dog race.

They were the Samaritans, and they were half-breeds. Jews didn't hang out with Samaritans because of this. They walked around Samaria, and they wouldn't dare to be caught in Samaria. The Samaritans worshiped in their area, and the Jews worshiped in their area. They didn't intermingle. Does this sound like our segregated worship on Sunday mornings?

So, here is Jesus saying, "I **need** to go through Samaria." He begins His journey to the Samaritan dogs. Jesus is always pushing us past traditions and ideas that hinder our relationship with Him. He passes the cultural mindset here and challenges man's perceptions. The Jews had closed minds and argued with Him saying, "This is the way we have done it. This is the way we are as Jewish people. We are Abraham's sons and daughters." Jesus rose up and responded, "I'm going to Samaria."

Many of us still believe the black church should be meeting over here, and the white church ought to be meeting over there, and we sure don't need to be intermingling together. Most will not actually say this out loud, but our actions reveal our hearts. They live in their part of town, and we live in our part of town. We all do our own thing. See, that's just the way we've been. The black church does this, the white church does this, and the Hispanic church does that. This is what tradition has taught us. Tradition says, "This is the way we worship." It amazes me how we try to determine how God should run His church by our desires and ignore what the Word says He wants.

Now we get to the part of the story where Jesus comes to the city of Sychar[48] to Jacob's well. He could have just said a well, but He identified it. He let us know, "Listen, this place is important." He not only tells us where it is, he says to us very clearly, this was Jacob's well. This was the ground that Jacob gave to his son Joseph. We can go back and trace this in the Old Testament to see exactly where it took place. He went to this well on purpose for He was being directed by the Father. I love this next verse.

[6]Now Jacob's well was there. Jesus therefore, being wearied from His journey, sat thus by the well. It was about the sixth hour. [7]A woman of Samaria came to draw water. Jesus said to her, "Give Me a drink."

That's not good. A Jewish man is going to touch a Samaritan's cup and drink from it? Jews don't even walk through there, let alone eat or drink with them. Communicate with them? This is not the way it is supposed to be.

[8]For His disciples had gone away into the city to buy food. [9]Then the woman of Samaria said to Him, "How is it that You being a Jew, ask a drink from me, a Samaritan woman?"[49]

She knew Jesus was a Jew. Isn't it sad that if you go to a white church, there is a white Jesus with blonde hair and blue eyes? Then you go to a black church and there is a

black Jesus with an afro. Let me say boldly that Jesus was a
Jew! Guess how she knew that He was Jewish? He certainly
didn't wear a sign that said Jew. You could tell by His
appearance, dress, language, and actions. Jesus was Jewish,
and it was obvious to all who saw Him.

If I came walking in, you could tell I'm a little white
short man with a little bit of a belly and a weird hairdo. I
may think I'm black, but it's easy to tell that I'm not. The
woman at the well knew! She is thinking *what are you doing
here? You would dare to ask me for a drink?* I don't understand what you're doing here, and you want my cup? These
details are important. I want you to understand something
about when Jesus stopped at Jacob's well.

I am going to give you some principles:

Start On Common Ground.

Our problem today is that we are divided, and we are
building on that division instead of focusing on unity. There
is something significant about meeting at Jacob's well. It was
a place each of them could identify with because, first, the
Jews knew that the covenant had been cut with Abraham,
Isaac, and Jacob. Second, the Samaritan people believed the
Pentateuch, and so they also honored Jacob. It was a place
they both could identify with. They both honored Jacob. He
met her at a place where they could have unity. He brought
her to a spiritual place where they could have identity and
common ground.

The only way we will build a multicultural church is by coming to a common ground. Most division starts with disagreement, but Jesus started with where they agreed. The other amazing thing is that Jesus didn't give up who He was to reach her. He didn't go into town and buy Samaritan clothes and try to look like a Samaritan to reach her. He was Jewish, and He knew who He was. He wasn't going to give up who He was. I don't have to act like you or look like you, but we are going to do this on our common ground. I'm disappointed when church leaders say they will only reach people like themselves. That's not true. We will reach who we love. That's who we will reach.

Celebrate Who You Are.

He did not deny who He was. He did not say, "Hey, I'm color blind." He knew who He was, she knew who He was. God is not asking you if you're black to like Country Western music. God is not asking us to be color blind. If God made you six feet tall with blonde hair, and your skin is as white as snow, then celebrate who you are. We will celebrate in our diversity, but we will be unified in Christ, our common ground. We celebrate one another's culture. We'll celebrate who we are. Our diversity shares God's glory.

He doesn't want us to be clones. Many churches want to make us clones. When you come into some churches, you have to look like them, act like them, carry your bible like them, talk like them. "Yes, Brother, Hallelujah!" You don't talk like that at home, but you get into the church and everybody does it. We have this church talk and church walk, and we go to this church and we all look alike. We all wear ties and we all do the same thing. Instead, we need to celebrate our diversity.

We need to celebrate that we are red, yellow, black or brown! We need to be excited about those things that diversify us. Diversity makes us powerful. Diversity shows God. God didn't want me to be a 6'10" guy who could dunk the ball. (It wouldn't have hurt my feelings.) He wants me to celebrate who I am. God wants you to be who you are as long as it doesn't interfere with the spiritual side of things. If we are celebrating white power and black power, then we have missed the principle and we've missed the whole thing.

I visited the Civil Rights Memorial and museum, and I stood at the pulpit of the 16th Street Church[50] in Birmingham, Alabama. This is where four little girls were killed by three white members of the Ku Klux Klan. These men took nine sticks of dynamite and stuck them under the staircase where they knew the little kids were having children's church. While the parents were in the sanctuary worshiping, they blew up the children's church, and four little girls were slaughtered.

As you looked at the pictures, the greatest thing about the Civil Rights movement was that there were white people involved. It wasn't a black thing. It was a freedom thing. We're all equal. It's not a Hispanic thing. We are all equal. This is not pro-black power. We are all equal. We are all one. We all deserve the same rights. We all deserve the same freedoms.

We all deserve the same chances. There were a lot of white people who died during the Civil Rights Movement.[51] If you look at the March on Washington, every culture was represented, that's what made it powerful. That's why it worked.

Our Christian Identity Supersedes Our Culture.

The spiritual is important here. Jesus is breaking His culture here. The church has an idea that we should stay separated because of our culture, but I'm telling you that's demonic, and that's tradition. That's not what the church should look like. Jesus said in John 17 the world will never know that God sent Him until His people are united. I guarantee when we do this thing, and do it right, they will ask what is it about the Church that they have every culture, every language, every nation, and every tribe? What makes us unified? Then we will have a voice to say, "It's Jesus."

You will see it happen. People desire it. They are tired of the racism that's going on. Our daddies were wrong. Our grandpas were wrong. I love my grandpa and grandma, but they missed the mark on racism. They were taught wrong, and they believed a lie. I'm not trying to be demean to them, but it's ok to stand up and say they were wrong. Alex Haley has been quoted as saying, "Racism is taught in our society, it is not automatic. It is learned behavior toward persons with dissimilar physical characteristics." Given that racism is a learned behavior it can also be changed. The power of the gospel is that lives change. We can't let stereotype mindsets affect us. Red, yellow, black or white, we are precious in His sight.

Let's return to the account in John 4 about the Samaritan woman. Jesus opened the door of conversation with her by saying He would drink from her cup. He first was in a place that was on common ground, and then He said, "Let me drink from your cup." So He's identifying with her, and she doesn't feel like He's saying, "I'm better than you." He was allowed to get into her business because He first identified with her.

Don't you hate it when someone tries to get in your business thinking they're better than you, and they never really identified with you or cared about you? Before you get into my business, you better understand me and you better care for me. If you care for me and love me, I'll let you into my business. However, if you don't care for me, don't even try. That is not going to work. Don't come judging me and condemning me until you can identify with me. Once you identify with me then you can speak to me.

It's so important to identify with one another. That's where Jesus had His open door to begin to talk with this lady. He said, "Let me drink of your cup." I love verse 10. Jesus is so smooth. She knew they were called Samaritans dogs. He said, "Hey, I don't call you a dog, I want a drink from your cup. Hey, we're friends here, we're breaking bad traditions." Remember now, where were the disciples? Yeah, they were buying food somewhere.

[10]Jesus answered and said to her, "if you knew the gift of God, and who it is who says to you, 'Give Me a drink," you would have asked Him, and He would have given you living water."[52]

Jesus knew how to slip right in. He knew how to move from the natural to the spiritual. He started with the physical and ended up in the spiritual. If we enter a conversation we first have to identify with the people and love them. That's why the days of going and knocking on doors just does not work in modern day evangelism. Some will disagree with my statement on door-knocking as a strategy for evangelism.[53] I will agree the approach is the key. You can't go up to someone and say, "You're going to Hell." God forbid! Honestly, we're probably not going to reach anybody like that.

We have to build relationships and friendships with the people we work with. We have to show them we care first. Do you know that's how Jesus reached people? He cared for them. He didn't act like them. He went and loved them and knew they were hurting. If we would do that, we could reach people. Don't be a bible-thumper and start reading a bunch of scriptures without starting out loving someone first. It is horrible. How many of you have experienced encounters with a few bible-thumpers that you couldn't stand? Did that drive you nuts? Many people have been driven away by a few bible-thumpers quoting scriptures at them. People don't care how much we know until they know how much we care first.

¹¹The woman said to Him, "Sir, you have nothing to draw with, and the well is deep. Where then do you get that living water?" ¹²"Are you greater than our father?

She says, "Our father." Notice she identified with Him. He identified with her, and she knew it and felt it! This allowed her to open up to Him.

¹³Jesus answered and said to her, "Whoever drinks of this water will thirst again, ¹⁴"but whoever drinks of the water that I shall give him will never thirst. But the water that I shall give him will become in him a fountain of water springing up into everlasting life."

And she said, "Sir, give me this drink. Let me have it." By doing so, she acknowledged that she was hurting, and she said, "I'm willing to take this."

¹⁶Jesus said to her, "Go, call your husband,

Uh oh, now the conversation has gotten deep. This is a family affair. "Go get your husband," and she's thinking, "Oooohhh!" Jesus always has a way of getting to the root. That's why when you're praying, and you're trying to tell God, "Change this person," or "Change that person," or "Do this," He first starts speaking to you and saying, "What about when you thought this, and what about when you acted like that?" Then you say, "Whoa...but Lord, what about this person?" The Lord always takes you back. Don't judge another until you deal with yourself. This is the fastest prayer you will ever get answered. If you don't believe God answers prayers just say, "Lord, show me where I'm messing up," and He'll answer your prayer by tomorrow, I promise.

*[17]The woman answered, "I have no husband." Jesus said to her, "You have well said, I have no husband,' "for you have had five husbands, and the one whom you now have is not your husband, in that you spoke truly." And the one you have now is not **even** your husband.*

Isn't it amazing that at this point Jesus addresses her sin? He was given room because He identified with her. That allowed Him to be able to talk to her.

[19]The woman said to Him, "Sir, I perceive that You are a prophet."

Well, I guess so! He just read into her life. When Jesus speaks into us, it turns on the light inside. The question is, will we respond?

[20]"Our fathers worshiped on this mountain and you Jews say that in Jerusalem is the place where one ought to worship."

This is a racial statement. Now wait a minute here, even though you're a prophet, you people do it over there, and we do it over here. Your churches do this, and we do that. This is the way we have always done it. This is the way it is. This is a historical position. If we read the history about this well, we will see that right behind her is Mount Gerizim.[54] She says,

"This is the mountain we've always worshiped at but you Jews, you worship at a *different* mount." Let the white people stay over there and worship, and let the black people stay over here and worship, and let's just keep our segregation.

The things that were done when they tried to desegregate the schools were absolutely wrong. The first black child who was going to go to one of the Montgomery schools was beaten.[55] Grown white men beat a little black boy and his father because this is the way we've always done it. We're not going to mess with tradition. We must be careful what we let tradition become. Be careful when you come into the church, and you say, "I think we ought to do it like this." Why? Because that's what your tradition taught you? Where did we get that idea we should do it like that? Because that's the way it's always been? What if the way you've always done it was wrong? Find the Bible and see what it says to you about your worship. Not about what your parents taught you or what your parents' parents taught you or what your tradition taught you, but what God wants to teach you.

See, we should be having a progressive revelation. That means the Word of God doesn't change, but we come to a greater understanding of the Word, and we grow deeper in the Lord. We grow closer to the Lord, and we understand things that they didn't understand years ago. The time is now for the multiracial church to stand up and raise her voice and say, "No more racism!" When Martin Luther King Jr. said, "I have a dream."[56] I have a dream that the little black boys and the little white boys will be as brothers; they will walk together, and they will worship together.

Still today, the most racially segregated day of the week is Sunday. Somebody has to raise his or her voice. The Church has to raise her voice and say, "No more! We're not going to do that stuff anymore." We are going to be the fulfillment of that dream and share the vision. The excuses from Christians saying, "This has been our culture, our tradition. It's been in our family a long time," must change. We are hindering Christ's church by staying segregated. If we don't change, we will lose many, we could have reached.

I have the greatest mom in the world, and I love her dearly! She has been faithful to me and sacrificed many things in life for me, but there are some things she has taught me and did that were goofy. Some of those things just had to change. My mom taught me that if I ever came to Indianapolis and got on I-465, the loop around Indianapolis, I'd never get off of it. Why? It is because she came to Indianapolis one time, got on I-465, and drove around it about 4 or 5 times. Then she got off and drove an hour and a half back home because she couldn't get off of the interstate.

So when I was sixteen years old and had my driver's license, I came to Indianapolis, and I was scared to death to get on I-465 because I thought I may never get off. Someone had to say to my mom, "That's wrong, it's real easy, just look at the signs." Sometimes when something is new we don't navigate it well. However, after we learn, we realize the advantages. The same is true about navigating the church into unity with every tribe, tongue, and race.

21Jesus said to her, "Woman, believe Me, the hour is coming when you will neither on this mountain, nor in Jerusalem, worship the Father."

Jesus is saying that there is a day coming when your tradition will mean nothing. We're going on past that tradition. However, the day will come when we're going to have a deeper relationship with the Lord. We're going past where we were. We're going to keep growing.

22You worship what you do not know; we know what we worship, for salvation is of the Jews." 23"But the hour is coming, and now is, when the true worshipers will worship the Father in spirit and truth; for the Father is seeking such to worship Him.

However, the hour is coming when true worshipers will worship the Father in spirit and in truth, not by culture and tradition. It is time that I find out how I need to worship, when I need to worship, what I need to worship, what the Bible says, and not just what tradition taught me. I need to listen to what the Bible says about worship. However, maybe the white church has always done it like that, and maybe the white church was *wrong* in doing it like that. You may say I like it that way. Well, worship is not about you but HIM. Some say you have to wear a tie when you come into God's

House. A church is actually not even God's House, *you* are God's House.

Some have said we should wear our very best when we go to church. If you want to that is fine; the problem is when we force everyone else to do as we do. We put our personal convictions not found in the word on others. Some have not attended church because they were unable to dress up and went into eternity never hearing the truth of Christ. Think about this, they miss the message because of what we thought they should wear! We have so many traditions that cultures have taught us that we see them as the gospel. Some of them are sacred cows that need to be shot, given a good burial, and we move on. I have heard Rick Warren say multiple times, there is nothing worse than riding a dead horse. Dismount he says, celebrate the good ride then give it a nice burial and move on with the Lord.

Consider this. Some people think that if there isn't screaming and shouting and people running around that they haven't had church. Well, you did a bunch of hooping and did you learn anything? On the other hand, some churches are so dead and so quiet that you're proud of yourself that you didn't go to sleep. I'm serious! I can remember going to church and being proud of myself that I didn't go to sleep. I even thought that God was happy with me because I stayed awake throughout the whole service.

I've watched some crazy things on TV and heard some crazy things from preachers. I have watched some churches hooping and going crazy, and I'm sitting in the living room saying, "What just happened?" Someone from that televised church might say, "I don't know what happened, but that's the way we've always done it, so that's the way we have to continue to do it." The day is coming when we will not worship like that. I love how Jesus brings this out in the next verse.

> [21]*Jesus said to her, "Woman, believe Me, the hour is coming when you will neither on this mountain, nor in Jerusalem, worship the Father."*

This is what He's saying, "Woman, the time is coming when God will only go to church where they are worshiping in spirit and truth, and if they are not worshiping like that, My Father won't be there. There may be a bunch of people, there may be a big building, there might be a bunch of noise going on, but if it's not being done in spirit and in truth, it's not where the Father is, because the Father is going to be where they are worshiping in spirit and in truth." The truth is not about tradition or culture. God is a Spirit; He's not material. Spirit means a right heart, a right attitude, while truth means right information. It is not the way you like it.

Can I be honest with you? Worship service was not made for you to come in and listen to the music you like so you can be happy, and you will be blessed. When did you get that idea that's what worship was about? I thought worship service was about coming to give **Him** glory and praise and honor. "But that's not the way I like to do it." It's not about you. It's not about your culture; we died to that. It's not about Jews and Gentiles; we died to that. It's not about being American, we've died to that, but we are one in Christ.

It's no longer my culture, I identify with. It's my Christianity. It's no longer my ideas or my friends I identify with, it's my faith. It's no longer my family tradition, I identify with, it's my faith. I died to tradition. I now live in my spiritual life. I am a Christian above all things in my life. Christianity is not coming to church sitting there and raising your hand, and throwing some money in the offering basket and then walking out and living like a heathen in the world. That's not Christianity. I know the churches may be packed doing that, but that's not Christianity. That's religion, that's culture, that's tradition. When we do church like that, we miss our opportunity to commune with God in a fresh and living way.

> [25]*And the woman said to Him, "I know that Messiah is coming" (who is called Christ). "when He comes, He will tell us all things."*[57]

Listen closely to what she's saying, "I listened to the prophecy series, I know the Messiah is coming, I have heard all about that, I have heard about Him."

> [26]*Jesus said to her, "I who speak to you am He."*

Now remember what I said about verse 8, about where the disciples went? They went to town to buy food.

> [27]*And at this point His disciples came and they marveled that He talked with a woman; yet no one*

said, "What do You seek?" or, "Why are You talking with her?

They came walking up (after walking miles to the nearest fast food restaurant) with food for them and Jesus. To their dismay they find Jesus there talking to this Samaritan Dog. They say, <whisper> "What in the world is He doing?" "Can you believe this?" It's not that she's a woman because He's already healed the woman with the issue of blood, and they didn't throw a fit about that. He's also been talking and hanging out with Mary and Martha, and they weren't upset with that. It must have been that she was Samaritan. It makes you wonder why Jesus had sent them away to buy food. Probably, because they were racist, and He knew He would never reach her with a bunch of racist people standing around.

We've had many people come to our church and say they want to be a part, but deep down, they have racism, and they leave. Many whites walk in hearing all sorts of good things going on at church. However, when greeted by black people, issues start arising in their hearts. Alternatively, black people, come in seeing the church grow only to see some whites in leadership, and they run in fear. Don't be fooled, terrible racism issues live in Christians. It is learned behavior passed down from generation to generation. Prejudging someone because of the way they look. How can it be among us?

People think blacks are lazy, inferior, or dangerous, and whites are racist and trying to keep the Black man down. I will boldly tell you, if you cannot love your brother or your sister, you cannot love God.[58] If you have racism in your heart you need to grow up, and you need to get on your knees and repent before God Almighty. Stereotyping, especially as Christians, is wrong. There are people of every race that are rude, mean and crude, and will hurt you. However, as a Christian we should love one another, and we need to get rid of all the stereotypes.

We should know that we need to reach the whole world and help them and love them. Maybe people wouldn't do the things they do if we would love them and help them and encourage them. Here's a piece of wisdom: hurt people, hurt people. Somebody who has been wounded will probably try to hurt you because that's what they know. That's why we (the church) are a hospital; we heal people. We should take people's lives and change them by the power of Jesus Christ.

[30]*Then they went out of the city and came to Him.*
[31]*In the meantime His disciples urged him, saying, "Rabbi, eat."*

He does one of those things that He always does, and He says, "I have food to eat that you do not know." You'd think it would have been fun walking with Him. This is one of these things where He's God, and He's Man, and this statement just makes no sense to them. If I went and bought you food then came back, and you wouldn't eat, I would also ask what happened. Did someone beat us back here and give

Him food? What happened while we were gone and who fed Him? They were also scared to say anything.

> [33]*Therefore the disciples said to one another, "Has anyone brought Him anything to eat?"*[59] [34]*Jesus said to them, "My food is to do the will of Him who sent me, and to finish His work."* [35]*"Do you not say, ' There are still four months and then comes the harvest'? Behold, I say to you, lift up your eyes and look at the fields for they are already white for the harvest!*

They must be thinking, what does the harvest have to do with the food we brought today? Wouldn't you have thought that? Lord, we're talking about lunch here not about the harvest!

> [36]*"And he who reaps receives wages, and gather fruit for eternal life, that both he who sows and he who reaps may rejoice together."* [37]*"For in this one saying is true: 'One sows and another reaps.'* [38]*"I sent you to reap that for which you have not labored; others have labored, and you have entered into their labors."*

They are probably thinking *we just asked you about lunch, that's all we said!*

> [39]*And many of the Samaritans of that city believed in Him because of the word of the woman who testified, "He told me all that I ever did."*

Now wait a minute, woman. He only told you how many husbands you ever had, and that He has water you haven't been able to drink before. However, she goes and tells the men. She already has a "man" problem, but what He said was so alive in her, she tells the men, and they say, "Take us to Him." The greatest thing about this is that it shows that no matter how much you have screwed up, you can still be a vessel unto God.

Maybe you have really flopped and messed up your life, this lady did too, but it was not too late. He still used her. He was at the same time drawing her. He still reached out to her. So the last thing he said to the disciples was, "look up, for the harvest is white", so they look up and what do they see? A woman walking along side of men whom the Jewish people considered to be half-breeds. They came walking and He said, "There is the harvest." No longer will we only reach the Jews.

I pray you will stop and meditate on that for a minute. No longer will we reach only our kind, but the harvest will consist of all men from every nation. There are people desiring a multi-cultural church and know that it's the right thing, but they are scared to say anything. It's up to us! I am just saying to you today to lift up your eyes because the harvest is plentiful. They are all around us. They are hurting and wounded and many feel isolated. They are destroyed and dismayed. They think God is mad, and that He hates them. We have to go identify with them, drink of their cup, and love them. We have to reach out to them.

[40]So when the Samaritans had come to Him, they urged Him to stay with them; and He stayed there two days. [41]And many more believed because of His own word.

He says the harvest is ripe and then there are these men. Then he goes and stays with them, and they get saved. Isn't it amazing? If he had followed tradition, He should have not even walked into that area, let alone had fellowship with these "half breeds;" and then goes and stays with them. We need to rethink our traditions and what we have been taught.

Maybe you have enjoyed the way we have done things, but we need to be honest and ask, is it in spirit and in truth? The context of this story is clear that Jesus is, for the first time telling them this is more than a Jewish thing. Let's change our mindset. The harvest is global and now at our back door.

HOW WE OVERCAME

CHAPTER SIX

OUR STORY

After a yearlong ordeal of arguing with God about planting a church (I didn't want to), my wife and I finally stepped out in faith. I tell people that I could write a book on how not to plant a church and sell a million copies. I did everything wrong that you possibly could. The only positive thing going for me was a building permit from God.

PSALM 127:1
Unless the Lord builds the house, They labor in vain who build it...

Don't get me wrong, my motives and heart were right, but my techniques and methods were substandard. After a couple of years of struggling, we rented a building in the city of Indianapolis and grew from 2 to 30 white people. When you start with a church of two people worshiping in your basement, while growing to the point of renting a building and attendance increasing to 30 people, you don't want it to fall apart at the seams.

One day while walking out the front door of the church, I noticed a multiracial couple walking down the road. My first thought was, *what is this neighborhood that we have moved into?* Now you can say that was a racist statement, yet I, like most whites would say I'm not racist. I really did not have anything against any other races, but I was like most white people and had never studied the Bible to see what God has to say about the races. This type of thought also exists in many black people. Some blacks have gone as far as claiming the Holy Scriptures as "The White Man's Bible."[60] They obviously have never studied it either. Both thoughts will be studied in detail in later chapters in this book.

While working on some school papers on racism I asked some pastors and many church leaders if they had ever studied racism from a biblical view point. The answer, no, was consistent with everyone. My studies and research absolutely shocked me and began to challenge my theological views. I began to see things such as God made Adam (which in the Hebrew means reddish) and made his body out of dirt. For the first time in my life, I began to think about race. Could it be that Adam was not as white as I had always assumed?

What color is God and did He make Adam look like Him? Kelly Varner said, "The truth always brings glory to God. The first man was neither black nor white. He was made from dirt, which can be a variety of colors, brown, black, dark, dusty, or sandy. He was probably reddish brown, as his name indicates."[61] These statements were hard to digest to thirty white people in our small congregation. Yes, I became so convicted and amazed at the churches lack of understanding that I started teaching it. We as Christians must open our hearts to allow the Holy Spirit to speak to us and even stretch us in what we thought we knew.

"It is interesting that a Black Adam and Eve appeared on the cover of the January 11, 1988 issue of Newsweek magazine."[62] Scott Bradley points out, "Biologically it has been proven that a black man, when mated with his kind, can produce a lighter skin toned baby, but a white man, when mated with his own kind, because of recessive genes in his genetic makeup, cannot produce a darker child. This would show that, biologically, it would have been impossible for Adam to have been a Caucasoid. All of mankind that came from him would possess that recessive gene, and that would make it impossible to produce a Negroid. To put it simply, light can come from dark but dark cannot come from light."[63] How do we as Christians respond when our views are challenged? Do we really base our beliefs on the truth of scripture or on our life long presumptions?

This is just the beginning of what the Bible has to say and how He began to challenge me in scripture and from this point forward my life and ministry began to change. I became consumed with the issue of racism, and my teaching would never be the same. I never gave thought to what would happen next. Yes, the worst possible event that could happen to a new church planter happened. Half of the people (15 white people) left the church. My heart was crushed, and I began to cry out to God, "Why did this happen?"

As Christians we must realize God will use our mess as a message, and our test will become testimonies. It was at this time in my life where I began to hear the Holy Spirit say to me, "I want you to build a multicultural church." I had no idea how to do it, the struggles we would go through doing it, the persecution, the rejection, and last of all, the glory we would bring to Christ by building a church that looks like heaven. We were told it couldn't be done, it would never work, and that we would fail. We were told it was not God's will, and it wouldn't last.

Now fifteen years later we have more than 1200 adults in our congregation with 30 nations represented. We have an ethnic blending of cultures from all over the world. The greatest thing about this is we have just begun. Now people come and say, "How are you doing it?"

Our Stories Of Struggles

One couple in our church tells the story, of how they never paid attention to the exclusiveness of their former church until their daughter became pregnant by a man from another race. They said that they saw and heard things from so- called Christians they could not believe. How would your church react? Alternatively, could I ask how would you feel if your daughter married a man of another race?

Another church member tells the story, of how she first came to church. "I loved the message, worship, authenticity, and most of all the presence of the Lord. I felt the Holy Spirit wanting me to be a part of this ministry, but as a black woman, I couldn't have a white pastor." Could you sit under the authority of someone who's a different race than you, what would your friends, your family, or your co-workers say?

CHAPTER SEVEN

OUR STEPS

I believe there are three distinctive steps that must be reached and maintained for a church to really be multicultural. These are the beginning levels of becoming diverse, and it must go deeper to integrate completely into the life of the church. We will then discuss additional components to help build or integrate a multicultural church.

1. **The congregation must be at the very minimum no more than 80% of one racial group.**

Most will define a multicultural church "as a church in which no one racial group makes up more than 80% of the attendees in one of the major worship services."[64] I argue that it must go much deeper.[65] A white church with a few blacks intermingled cannot be referred to as multicultural or vice versa. The church has failed so miserably in the area of multicultural congregations; we have celebrated one or two couples of a different ethnic group, in a church of one hundred as being multicultural. The world would be swift to call us out on those assumptions. When the ratios are balanced, it's easy to see the authenticity. **We must be careful not to use a minority group as a token of success.**

2. The elders and deacons must be multicultural.
This is a highlight of the multicultural church and a sure sign of accomplishment. The Antioch church which celebrated its diversity of leadership became the sending church to the nations and the focus of the Holy Spirit in Acts thirteen.

3. The paid staff of the church must be multicultural.
These first three items are the measuring stick of evaluation for the multiracial churches' progress. Items two and three are critical for the issues of church power. This issue of power is rarely discussed in an open, honest discussion among people who want to integrate, but it speaks loudly through its action. Most will agree racism is to some degree, at its root, about power.[66] Many have defined racism as racial prejudice plus power. I would agree that this is a good working definition to start with. "To be anti-racist involves not only the elimination of racial prejudice among individuals, but also moving with intentionality to dismantle the systems of power that support racial disadvantages within societal structures and institutions. To be anti-racist calls for a shift and sharing of power dynamics, which historically has created power and powerless groups based on race or ethnicity."[67]

I have found the only way a minority group will feel totally at home is when the voice of power is shared. Especially minorities, as they enter a church, must see that they again are not walking into oppression. When they see that the voice of power is shared and heard, their fears are silenced. The World Council of Churches states that: "To be the church today requires an effort to overcome racism through actions to transform society and its structures of power and exclusion."[68]

This becomes a huge open door for all races to come in and feel welcome. It speaks so loudly that it becomes major reason people will make your church their home. Let me reiterate that all three points must take place to build a multicultural church with a solid foundation.

To start a multicultural church from the beginning, this is a positive road map and vision marker to judge the progress. To attempt to make changes in an existing congregation, these steps must be taken gradually. Many of the steps discussed later will need to be focused on at first in an existing congregation.

As much as I have come to realize the necessity of the first three steps, there are a few warnings I must declare. Do not hire, ordain, choose, or vote on a board member, deacon, or staff member just because they are a different culture. You must make sure they have the multicultural vision, and the calling to fulfill such a critical role. The Bible is clear in defining qualifications of elders and deacons. Study 1 Timothy 5, Titus 1, 1 Peter 5, and 1 Timothy 3.

1 TIMOTHY 5:21-22

[21]*I charge you before God and the Lord Jesus Christ and the elect angels that you observe these things without prejudice, doing nothing with partiality.* [22]*Do not lay hands on anyone hastily, nor share in other people's sins; keep yourself pure.*

4. **The worship team and music must be multicultural.**

When people come into the church, worship is many times what is frequently seen and heard at the beginning of service. When visitors listen and observe your worship team, what is being said about your stance on racism? The music style of one ethnic group must not be allowed to dominate the worship that plays from the platform every Sunday. Worship speaks volumes and is instrumental in reaching every culture.

There is power in music and it creates atmosphere. Many examples in history demonstrate this truth. David Tame, a musicologist, writes, "Throughout the ages wise men have noted music's profound impact on its listeners. For example, over 2000 years before the birth of Christ, the musical systems of China were highly developed in to its society. It was to this that the philosophers directed much of their attention. Understanding its intrinsic power, they carefully checked their music to make sure that it conveyed eternal truths and could thus influence man's character for the better."[69]

In addition, music can be used to subvert as well. Vladimir Lenin, the cofounder of communism and one of history's greatest experts on subversion and revolution, said one quick way to destroy a society is through its music. Music is not only that powerful, but it also creates an atmosphere. It can make you feel good, sad, excited, rowdy, etc. Most people are also very sensitive and feel emotionally loyal to the music they enjoy.

So if a white person comes to church and only hears gospel or black music, they usually won't feel comfortable. I will define white music as instrument-led and black music as voice-led for this book. Using all white worship and expecting blacks to engage is a mistake. You can say as a church, we are open to all nations, but your choice of music speaks for itself. A key to thriving in a multicultural setting is a mixture of music. DeYoung agrees with me and went on to say it also provides a completepicture of God.[70]

When we started, we would have the worship team do a couple of black gospel songs and also a couple of white worship songs. This was one reason many said a multicultural church would never work. One man said, "Well, I don't listen to a white music station and switch to a black station." That was a good point and caused me to go to the Lord in prayer. During this time, I began to realize that every new move of God always seemed to carry a new sound with it.

Great revivals with Jonathan Edwards, Charles Finney, George Whitefield, William Seymour and many more carried a refreshing, and new sound to the church. God led forth many in scripture in new seasons with a new sound; Genesis 3, Leviticus 23, Numbers 10, Joshua 6, 2 Chronicles 29, Joel 2, Matthew 24, Acts 2, 1 Corinthians 15, Revelation 4, Revelation 8, and Revelation 19. This list is not exhaustive or meant to be doctrinal. Every generation in the world also carries with it a new sound. So how about the multicultural church carrying with it a new sound? We at the Blended Church began to believe God for a multicultural sound in our services.

We also see this now happening within the Church, with artists such as Israel Houghton, Derick Thomas, and one of the first to produce multicultural worship, Ron Kenoly. "Houghton tells the story on worship as: 'When I started getting into the recording industry, I would hear, Choose a style, and I used to say, How about we just put it all together? Because when we get to heaven, there's not going to be sections—This is the black section of heaven. This is the white section of heaven. What kind of music do you like? Well you're going to be over in that room. I believe the Kingdom has a sound. I believe glory has a sound. So I want to be a part of doing it. I believe it's a very multi-cultural mix of sound and style and lyric and melody and everything else.'"[71]

We even see a new sound of worship was introduced by David in the Old Testament that led the people out of the worship of the law into the new life we should find in the church. "The Tabernacle of David is the name given to the tent that King David set up on Mount Zion in Jerusalem to house the Ark of the covenant. The Ark of the Covenant was originally housed in the Tabernacle of Moses (also called the Tabernacle of the Congregation). In the year 1050 B.C., David brought the Ark to Jerusalem and placed it in a tent, the Tabernacle of David (2 Samuel 6, 1 Chronicles 13-16). The Ark stayed in David's Tabernacle for 40 years until it was moved into the Temple built and dedicated by David's son Solomon in 1010 B.C. (2 Chronicles 5-7). The majority of the Psalms were originally sung as prophetic songs in David's Tabernacle.

They account in detail the expressions of worship offered by the Israelites before the Ark of the Covenant. It was the center of a new order of joyful worship, which stood in sharp contrast to the solemn worship of Moses' Tabernacle. Instead of the sacrifices of animals, the sacrifices offered at David's Tabernacle were of praise, joy and thanksgiving (Psalm 95:2,100:4, 141:2). The Tabernacle of David is a type of the worship of the Church. Jesus fulfilled the sacrificial system of the Old Covenant by His death on the cross (Hebrews 1:3, 7:27, 9:12, 9:24-28). The sacrifices of the Church, the New Covenant priesthood, are the sacrifices of praise, joy and thanksgiving (Hebrews 13:15, 1 Peter 2:9)."[72]

We at the Blended Church constantly teach on our vision and purpose. In doing so, we teach the people worship is not about them but God. We will do different types of worship to draw all people, and we then move to an area of a multicultural sound. We have grown as a worship team and even developed our own style of music that identifies the church. So, a key to be thriving as a multicultural church is the sound of the house. Let me reiterate and say you can't do exclusively one type of music and say all are welcome. The people will not feel that they or their needs are met.

One great tool we have found to mix up the sound is to have a black person lead out front in worship singing a white song, or a white person a black song. It's amazing the effects this has on the worship. One characteristic we see about the new breed of multicultural worshippers is, for instance, Thomas and Houghton leading worship with an acoustic guitar. A black man leading worship with an acoustic guitar breaks every mode. This has a deep impact on the worship.

Ethnomusicology is the study of cultural patterns and ethnic lifestyles that affect the music of each group. The wording comes from the Greek words ethnos (nation) and mousike (music). Damian Emetuche recognizes "that music is cultural and each ethnic group has its own musical style. From the colonial missionary endeavor of the 18th, 19th, and part of the 20th centuries, western missionaries had simply translated the old traditional hymns. It was almost the same tune, rhythm, and style from London to New York, Hong Kong to Mexico City, and from Lagos to Sao Paulo.

The colonial missionaries, because of their lack of interest in the culture of the people they were serving, imposed their musical style on the indigenous population. However, with the help of anthropology and ethnomusicology, we now recognize the difference in music style of different races and people groups. Because of the differences in style of music, it becomes extremely challenging for a multicultural church to determine the worship style to adopt. Frankly, the music style you like best says more about you –your background and personality –than it does about God. One ethnic group's music can sound like noise to another. Therefore, it becomes imperative that the worship style of a multicultural church has to be inclusive in nature. The music style of one ethnic or cultural group must not be allowed to dominate; elements of other cultures have to be factored into the worship."[73]

5. **The multicultural purpose and vision must be written and seen by every one who enters the building.**

It must be clear and easily accessible everywhere in the church. The book of Habakkuk teaches a powerful aspect of vision.

HABAKKUK 2:2

Then the LORD answered me and said: Write the vision And make it plain on tablets, That he may run who reads it.[74]

The vision has to be written so it can be read. Every vision goes through a degradation[75] process, so when we feel like quitting, we can go back and read what God has said to us. The degradation of a dream or vision is a part of the process of dreaming big. It happened in the life of Abraham, Joseph, David, Moses, Peter, etc. It's a part of a process to eternal significance.

Let everyone see the vision boldly and clearly. Habakkuk goes on to say:

"so he may run who reads it."

We can't run a race, unless we know which way to run, how many laps, etc. Writing it down keeps all of us on focus and allows us to see where we're going, and what it will take to get there. Vision must be taught often in all areas of the ministry of the church, including the pulpit. At our church, the purpose statement is out in our foyer area so all can see it and read.

The Blended Church

Our purpose is to live the word of God and proclaim it by:

◆ Exalting the Lord Jesus Christ in worship

◆ Evangelizing the unsaved

◆ **To unite people out of every tribe and tongue and people and nation (Rev 5:9)**

◆ Establishing Christians in intimacy with Jesus, in His Lordship and in personal holiness

◆ Equipping the saints for effective ministry

◆ Starting new churches and sending out missionaries

So all must know a part of the vision of the church is to bring all nations together. We have a racism wall that is in our foyer that cast the vision clear. This wall consists of huge historic photographs of multiracial people struggling for freedom in the Civil Rights Movement. These hang below a forty foot banner that reads: *Uniting Every Tribe, Tongue and Race. Rev 5:9.*

In addition we have a huge brick wall that runs between the buildings on our campus. It also has that Revelation 5:9 statement written on it with flags of every nation that we support. You cannot miss the vision of the church no matter where you're at on the grounds. We so celebrate our diversity it creates a huge momentum for the church. It also has a huge impact on visitors. Ninety percent of every guest who attends says they have never seen so many races worship together.

This fact alone brings a lot of people back for another visit and has caused many to turn to Jesus in faith. We have had newspaper and magazine articles written about us, because, celebrating diversity while worshiping in unity, brings the presence of the Lord, whom all can sense. Another powerful thing that has transpired when people see the races together, they leave forever changed. Never again do they walk in another church without noticing if there is a racial issue. When they experience the blending, you can't go back to segregation.

Our sign in front of our church has been one of the most amazing vision casting implementations we have. With the powerful testimonies it has created, it has also produced many persecutions.

The sign reads as follows:

◆ The Blended Church

◆ No Racism

◆ No Judging

◆ Just Jesus

This is actually a temporary sign that has remained in front of our present campus buildings for the last four years. It's a huge (15' tall x 8' wide) red banner that has become well known throughout the city. As ugly as it is (being a temporary banner) it has had an astonishing impact. Many people who have driven by have come to visit and have turned to Christ. We constantly hear people say "Oh, the church with the red sign that says, no racism." These reports come from people who live as far as forty five minutes away from the campus.

I have come to believe the No Racism statement has generated great thought to something we have glossed over. All people regardless of church attendees or not, when forced to think about it, realize the church has participated in racial segregation. It's very rare that an unbeliever will complain about the sign, but the response from other churches has amazed our church staff. Why have they complained? Are we personally attacking other churches, or a problem we feel exists? On this matter, I will let you judge.

6. Location.

Our church purposely bought and built in an area where both black people and white people would feel comfortable coming. Most metropolitan cities have had issues of white flight and the negative issues it brings up. White flight is the movement of many whites out of cities and into suburban areas. This trend was caused in part by fear of rising crime in cities, and in part by a sense that the quality of schools was falling in the wake of racial integration. Race riots in a number of large cities in the 1960s helped fuel white fears.

A similar trend by blacks was sometimes called "bright flight." Both trends had a serious impact, and contributed to a decline in the quality of city life and neighborhoods in these years.[76] Most neighborhoods have had some issues of racism arise from different families moving in or out. We chose an area that all ethnicity would feel welcome to enter. The location of the church speaks about the purpose and vision. If you have an existing building in an area that's not blended, it does not mean you can't build a multicultural church. However, when you do build this must be a huge part of your decision of where to build.

7. Multi Racial Appearance

When people first arrive at your church, what do they see? We briefly mentioned the visual aspect but let's look closer. First impressions are a major part of the visitor's decision if they will return or not. With racism living so prevalent among us, we must be aware of its effects. If a white person walks in and sees only black people at the door, this could cause them to start feeling fear or at least cause them to feel uncomfortable. The same is true for a black person walking in a church greeted by only white people.

This is a huge statement for a multicultural church to have people of different races at the door. This is something that everyone who enters our church speaks of. Please don't overlook this. If you walk in a store, restaurant, or church, and you are a different color than those in the building, you notice it. So what do the choices about your ushers and greeters say concerning racism? We actually make sure that in every area of the church, there is an integration of all colors of people.

Our greeters, ushers, children's church workers, worship team, and all leaders or workers who represent the church are strategically placed. Actions against segregation taken in every area speak louder than words. Too many churches say we are multicultural or open to it, yet when you enter the services nothing could be farther from the truth. Let it be seen loud and clear!!

8. A multicultural church must be done intentionally!

It must be a major part of the church's vision, and this is often overlooked. Charles Foster says, "Few congregations have been organized with the intention of embracing racial and cultural diversity."[77] He goes on to say, "Some discover new possibilities for their futures through the responsiveness to people who do not share their racial and/or cultural heritage."[78] While I agree some multicultural churches have started because of "white flight" they do not usually remain as such. Usually, once a change of power happens within the leadership, the race of the leader takes over. George Yancey says, "Predominantly white Christian churches frequently follow whites in their flight out of the neighborhoods of racial minorities.

It is fairly clear that many of these predominantly white mega churches have fled the inner cities much like other white institutions. Racial minorities, especially African Americans, are aware of the effects of white flight. They recognize how the fleeing of capital and resources from their communities has harmed their neighborhoods. They perceive predominantly white suburban churches as places not welcoming to them."[79] An example of this is demonstrated by a church leader (deacon) who told me his church was moving west of the city because blacks were taking over the city, and his church's leadership was not going to let that happen to the church. His church was close to ours, and he questioned how we could let this happen to our church. They are now in a white suburban area with a sign that says: All are welcome!

I will share the changes that have to be made intentionally so the church will thrive as a multicultural fellowship. Before I do that I want to address Foster's comment "that few have started or organized intentionally." I have personally spent time with pastors of multicultural congregations of *over one thousand* people and everyone has made very intentional organizational decisions to maintain diversity. I mention of over one thousand people because they are thriving and have less of a chance of digressing.

David Anderson agrees with my argument by saying, "Few churches become incidentally or accidentally multicultural due to the changing demographics in their community and those that do are prepared to handle the multiple problems that confront many of them, many of which could be avoided. Intentionally is critical as it enables one to leverage a multicultural vision ahead of the curve and provide a greater sense of direction. Intentionally equips the church to jump ahead of the pack instead of jumping on the bandwagon a day late and a dollar short. Intentionally is biblically mandated and culturally smart."[80]

Good leaders try to stay ahead of the vision. This allows you to move ahead instead of always just reacting to the problems. Curtiss Paul DeYoung takes the argument of intentionality one step further by arguing, "Intentionality is important because the social tendencies in the United States lean toward racial separation instead of integration. We have been taught subtle lessons about the importance of 'staying with one's own kind".

To overcome this propensity, it is important that the clergy and the laity of the church are consistently in active conversation about how they can create and maintain their multiracial makeup."[81] In the research of Scott Thumma and Dave Travis, authors of *Beyond Megachurch Myths,* it was revealed that many mega churches have intentionally adopted an inclusive vision and that has caused growth. Eighty five percent of the mega churches made changes in the worship and worked to recreate themselves to reach all groups of people.[82]

9. Yes, a price must be paid.

You must be willing to change the way you do things so the church can blend. It is not easy, and there will always be obstacles in the way. Change is always difficult to navigate through, but living and growing ministries must continue to grow. The "what if's" will never go away. Some may ask, "Is the timing right?" Timing is an important element, but of greater urgency is the voice of the Holy Spirit. When we choose to obey His voice, and step out into unknown waters, there is always a price to pay.

LUKE 14:28

For which of you, intending to build a tower, does not sit down first and count the cost, whether he has enough to finish it.

The World Council of Churches summed it up well: "To be the church today requires deliberate, consistent and constant action in the struggle for racial justice. To be the church today requires transformation into church communities, which fully live the diversity of their peoples and cultures as a clear reflection of God's Creation and Image in humankind. To be the church today calls churches to make a costly commitment to overcome their own division on racial-ethnic lines. To be the church today means overcoming racism by re-establishing right relationships with the churches' own people: women and men, Indigenous Peoples, Africans and peoples of African-descent, Dalits, and ethnic minorities. It means churches facing the truth of the life and death wrongs that they themselves perpetrated in the past against racially and ethnically oppressed peoples, as well as their acts of environmental racism. It is to search and tell the truth about the realities of racism as expressed in assimilation policies, superiority myths, disrespect to the diversity of cultures and identities, disrespect to creation. To be the church today is to be healing communities, transformed by the lives, gifts and spirits of their own people, and to uphold the interconnectedness of life as a whole."[83]

When someone steps out obeying God and pays a price for the actions of faith or obedience, it usually becomes a stepping stone into their future. The troubles that plagued us in the beginning have become a strong foundation today. It was the negative feedback, name calling, and people telling us we could not bring the races together that motivated us to do it. The struggles provided us a common rallying point to stand on in victory and shout: "Look what the Lord has done!"

10. Guest Speakers and Guest Musicians.

This becomes a great way to build momentum and show the multiracial vision from the platform. Maybe you have thirty white people and want to begin the thrust of blending the cultures. This is a great avenue of beginning the process without having different cultures in your church. Most people in segregated congregations have failed to realize how much they have missed not experiencing ministry from other cultures. Churches have used the terms full gospel in arguing over their stance on the Holy Spirit. Could it be we have all have missed the fullness of the gospel not experiencing the gospel from all nations, race and people? Ministry from another culture can be refreshing and produce new life in areas we have not known. Bring in guest speakers to preach on racism.

As a power stabilizer, our church reinforces the vision by continuously inviting speakers and musicians who are multi-cultural. If we bring in a black worship guest, we make sure the next time we bring in some other culture next time. The experiences have been an overwhelming success. The different preaching styles and different types of music deeply enhance the congregation.

I will never forget the experience of bringing in a guest named Obadiah. A few years ago, I invited a guest dramatist to perform for our Sunday services. The congregation only knew the drama involved a man named Obadiah, who made the nails that crucified Christ. He appeared on stage as an old black man. His skin was wrinkled, and his voice was crackled with a broken Louisiana Ebonic accent.

He told the story of the nails; the agony he felt knowing the nails he created, crucified the same man whom he walked with along the streets of Jerusalem. If he had known those nails would help kill the son of God, he would not have made them. The story focused on how we all had a part in putting the nails in. The very last scene, this older black man begins to unveil his real person. The reality is that this man, who stood before us for 45 minutes as an older black man, was a white man who could impersonate this character. He had blacks and whites taking deep breaths of shock as he unraveled the costume and make up. The reaction was shocking. The black people stood up and said no way! The white people were in a state of shock. The assumption that a person, who walks a certain way, speaks a certain way had fooled the entire congregation. What a lesson we learned that day on prejudging a person.

11. **Every outreach, mailer, article, phone book ad, web site, must have the multicultural message.**

Never take it for granted that people know what you're doing to break down the walls of racism. This is such a fresh approach to the ministry it must be included in every thought and action. We have used mailers quite regularly to get our message out. I have listed an example, and you can find some more examples on the book's website.

(A) The front had a picture of a group of multiracial babies while the picture next to it was of a cemetery. The wording said: There are only two times when it doesn't matter who your neighbor is.

(B) The back said: Have you ever dreamed of a place... Where you would be accepted as you are? Have you ever wished for people that would care for you... Regardless of the color of your skin? Do you have a desire to know God... But, you don't like or understand the old fashioned rituals at some churches? Have you ever wondered if there was a church... Where the teachings would come alive and have relevance in today's world? Where you would actually look forward to going to church!

Why The Blended Church?

- ◆ You've never experienced anything like this before.
- ◆ Exciting Worship!
- ◆ People from every tribe, nation, tongue, and race.
- ◆ Embracing every culture, celebrating our diversity.
- ◆ Messages that are relevant.
- ◆ Ministry for the Whole Family,
- ◆ Experience Jesus
- ◆ Casual Dress
- ◆ A Church that Looks Like Heaven.
- ◆ We are the church that will raise our voice in the last days. No more racism! • NO PREJUDICE, OR RACISM, JUST JESUS. If you've been looking for a multiracial church, you've just found it!

This flyer had a huge impact on people.

Web sites, Google ads, and billboards are all effective streams of communication. Newspapers are always looking for fresh stories, and a multicultural church fits that mode. Step out in faith and see how God will move in great ways.

12. Preach it from every platform you can.

When preaching and teaching the vision of the church, you need to do it as many different ways as possible. Someone said, "It's like fishing. You put as many lines in the water as possible to catch the most fish." So preach it in different ways every time you can. Find a way to mention it in your messages weekly. Use some of the stories in this book. One great avenue we have used is to use movie clips. There are some great movies of the struggles of racism along with some stories of people overcoming. We live in such a media driven society, using clips greatly enhances the emotions of the service. One great documentary to use is the story of The Class Divided. Here is a quick summary.

"On the day after Martin Luther King Jr. was murdered in April 1968, Jane Elliott's third graders from the small, all-white town of Riceville, Iowa, came to class confused and upset. They recently had made King their "Hero of the Month," and they couldn't understand why someone would kill him. So Elliott decided to teach her class a daring lesson in the meaning of discrimination. She wanted to show her pupils what discrimination feels like, and what it can do to people.

Elliott divided her class by eye color — those with blue eyes and those with brown. On the first day, the blue-eyed children were told they were smarter, nicer, neater, and better than those with brown eyes. Throughout the day, Elliott praised them and allowed them privileges such as a taking a longer recess and being first in the lunch line. In contrast, the brown-eyed children had to wear collars around their necks, and their behavior and performance were criticized and ridiculed by Elliott. On the second day, the roles were reversed and the blue-eyed children were made to feel inferior while the brown eyes were designated the dominant group.

What happened over the course of the unique two-day exercise astonished both students and teacher. On both days, children who were designated as inferior took on the look and behavior of genuinely inferior students, performing poorly on tests and other work. In contrast, the "superior" students — students who had been sweet and tolerant before the exercise — became mean-spirited and seemed to like discriminating against the "inferior" group. "I watched what had been marvelous, cooperative, wonderful, thoughtful children turn into nasty, vicious, discriminating little third-graders in a space of fifteen minutes, says Elliott."[84]

Testimonies and stories of church members also work well. There are stories that will amaze you if you ask around. One great thing I have learned is God will bring you key people to help you with the vision at the perfect time you need them.

THE PAST AND WHAT MUST BE CHALLENGED

CHAPTER EIGHT

THE INITIAL PROBLEMS

Billy Graham said "Without question, the single greatest social problem that faces our world is racism."[85] Why has the church not responded? Why have we not acted? Why is "Sunday morning still the most racially segregated day throughout the week?"[86] Until the church steps up and does something about it, we will continue to stifle the voice of the Lord Jesus Christ on the planet. After much research and fighting the issue of racism in the church daily for over fifteen years, I will attempt to show the reasons why the church has struggled.

Most churches say and feel they have no thread of racism in them. They say that they are open to all cultures, and as a matter of fact, they want to become multicultural. This comment presents many of the problems of racism in the church. There is a lot of talk, but very little action. Churches will say they want racism to go away, but the real question is what are they doing to make it go away? While lynching of slaves was taking place the church was silent. While train's filled with slaves traveled right by our churches, for the most part, the church continued to praise behind their walls but did not step out of them. When Adolph Hitler was murdering thousands of Jews, where was the church? When slave owners had black families stand up on a platform for sale, where was the church?

One major emphasis of this book is that the church has not taken action to fight against racism. It's also contributed with ignorance, myths, fear, a lack of biblical understanding, and just being comfortable with the status quo. Including thoughts that the government will make it go away, or there's nothing we can do about it. Another thought that must be addressed in the church is the "notion that there is no longer a serious problem of discrimination in the US society. From this perspective, it is frequently suggested that the 1960s civil rights laws and policies had taken care of most racial discrimination."[87] Civil rights was a reaction, not a solution.

I argue that racism has not improved in the church. I would say it has grown worse because of "racial fatigue," a hopelessness that it will never change and a mindset that we have no power to do anything about it. I cry out that the church must take action. "The church should take the leadership in the matters of justice and reconciliation. In some cases, we have failed to do so and have added to the problem rather than providing a solution. This display and apathy is in need of correction."[88]

The church is supposed to be the light of the world. However, we've been the taillights, not the headlights. It's time for the church to arise and put some action to our faith. "God is calling us to a redemptive perspective on ethnic relations. The fall of man has impacted every dimension of our thinking, especially ethnic issues. The timing in America's history couldn't be more strategic.[89] "It is rather ironic that the Christian church was a forerunner in the abolitionist and civil rights movements, yet remains one of the most segregated institutions in the contemporary society."[90]

Why has the church taken the back seat? We can do more. From the mature Christian to the one who just committed himself to Christ, we would all agree. Anthony Pinn takes it further by saying: "religion has been the most flagrant perpetrator of racism in the world. In particular the Christian Church in America has been the leader of racism in the world and particularly in America."[91]

Racism is a Kingdom agenda. This is about the Kingdom of God here on earth. This is not a black agenda or a white agenda. Black is only beautiful when it is biblical. White is only right when it agrees with the holy writ. Racism is not a problem of skin but a problem of sin and its preconceived ideas. If we keep it social, it won't change. However, if we deal with it spiritually, we can make a change. The church must take action.

The church and the people are supposed to know something about sin. Can we not recognize how subtle and deep this human demon is? Campolo makes a statement that rips at my heart while discussing unity. "In the Western Church human and unity is found in some kind of conglomerate heterogeneous persons bound together primarily by individualistic spirituality. In that view, there really is no unity in Christ, only convenient alliances between Christians. We still have the black church here and the white church over there. We must admit there is little unity, and only an accepted tolerance."

Do we really think racism has changed? Tony argues that, "Overt racism has in the past half-century, given way to a more subtle form of modern and internalized racism. Protestant denominations in the United States have developed anti-racism initiatives and encouraged their congregations to open themselves up to a greater racial diversity. However, the separation of the white church and a black church remains entrenched. Denominational initiatives often come across as mere lip service with a little commitment." No action allows racism to continue with in Christ's kingdom and within His body. We talk but do nothing of any significance.

JAMES 1:22:

But be doers of the word, and not hearers only, deceiving yourselves.

"The church needs to be healed of its poison of racism if it is to be a source of healing for a society. We must acknowledge that if Christians in the United States, and only

Christians, ceased participating in racism; this problem would be radically diminished in our churches, homes, and society."[92]

Two great points were made here. The first is the church needs healing if we are to be a source of healing for the society. The church is the answer to a sick society, but we have no voice if we also participate in the sickness. How can the church speak to the city when we look and participate in the sickness? The world and our cities are looking for answers but won't ask us for help until they see our fruit. Their philosophies have not worked, and they are spending millions on committees and investigating any solution.

The second point made by Raymond Blanks was if we, as the church alone broke down the walls it would significantly change everything around us. That statement by itself shows how bad racism lives in the church. As walls come down, we can see the difference we can make. The next thing we see is we can make a difference. We just have to step out, be willing to face our fears, and put our faith into action. A friend and a man who has taken great steps against racism, Dr. Charles Ware, said "the sad fact is the church has a greater conformity to the world than the word in the issues of segregation."

"The dirty little secret in America is that we are a racially segregated society, and we are comfortable in the segregation."[93] Many people feel that to admit to this comfort is to admit to being comfortable with racism, and we do not want to be perceived as racist. It usually takes us being confronted with the issue before we really dig deep into our souls to see if any thread of racism lives in us. How would you honestly feel about your children dating someone of another race? How would you feel if your pastor resigned and a new pastor of another race became your pastor? How would you feel about working for someone of another race? What about walking down the street alone and seeing someone of another race coming toward you? Racism hides deep in the heart and lives in the dark so as not to be exposed.

Our problem is we all think we are not at fault, it's not in us personally, and here are some of our excuses:

I'm not the cause.

I'm not a racist.

It's not my responsibility.

I don't live in a multicultural area.

I have friends that are both black and white.

I would if I could.

It's not my calling.

Have you ever heard yourself repeat one of these statements? Would you allow me to suggest that breaking racism is a commission from Jesus himself?[94] "Whites do not have to be overtly prejudiced, nor do they have to discriminate knowingly, for the structure of racism to persist."[95] The structure being referred to is white privilege. If people do nothing, the problem will continue to persist. Let me take this comment to the next level.

Blacks don't have to be overtly prejudiced, nor do they have to discriminate knowingly for racism to persist. Albert Einstein once said, "Insanity is doing the same thing over and over again and expecting different results."[96] My argument is clear, we must act. The white church must change; the black church must change. The church must admit its sin and be willing to change. Then we will have a voice.

My point is summed up best by Bowers when she said, "As congregations become more racially and ethnically diverse, they will transfer what they've learned in the church into the community."[97] Then we will have a clear voice to the world. "Proper analysis and confrontation are necessary to counteract and eradicate racism, bigotry, ethnocentrism and oppression."[98] So let's investigate our attitudes, ideologies, excuses, and traditions that are perpetuating the problem. Let's ask some questions that go to the root of the issue. Are whites superior to blacks or vice versa? Do whites or blacks have an advantage over each other? Is Christianity a white or black man's religion? What does the Bible say about the races? These are the real questions we will ask ourselves in the up and coming chapters. However, before we do, we have to tackle the word culture.

CHAPTER NINE

CULTURE

The focus on being political correct has diluted or simply confused the real issues of reconciliation. True reconciliation and unity come only in the redemptive work of Christ. The 2010 census has many asking, would I be multicultural, multiethnic or multiracial? In Australia, the census form asks about "ancestry" which gives a snapshot of the ethnic origins of the population. I must admit that's better. However, the purpose of this book is not to determine or define words we should use.

Terminology is constantly changing and attempting to redefine a word. We also have extreme or fringe groups attempting to hi-jack a word or movement. The word multicultural is a perfect example of discussion. Multicultural terms are defined as relating to or including more than one culture or ethnic group. This deals with ancestry, not sexual preference according to scripture. Same sex marriage proponents have attempted to say multicultural identifies their agenda. A movement from segregation to inclusion they proclaim. They have set about to expand the word multicultural to define tolerance and inclusion of that lifestyle. To put it simple, one does not determine to be white or black, but sexual preference is a choice.

So let's take a deeper look at the word culture and define it, so we can see the differences of culture and race. "The word culture, like the word religion, is very difficult to define. In one sense every different person is from a different culture. We each have our own symbol system and ways of defining the meaning of our life."[99] I personally like Lesslie Newbigin's definition, "To define the word culture we have to understand the sum total of ways of living developed by a group of human beings and handed on from generation to generation. This must include language. Central to the theme of culture is language. The language of the people provides the means by which they expressed their way of perceiving things and of coping with them."[100] To break it down in simple terms culture is how you grew up, who you grew up with, the way you learned, and who taught you; it differs from race. "Culture is the sum of attitudes, customs, and beliefs that distinguishes one group of people from another. Culture is transmitted through language, material objects, rituals, institutions, and art from one generation to the next."[101]

So how does race and culture differ? ABC News's page stated, "What the facts show is there are differences among us that stem from culture not race."[102] This concept is discussed further in the book One Blood: The Biblical Answers to Racism. It has changed the view of many concerning the issue of race. "The only reason many people think there are major differences in race is because they have been brought up in a culture that has taught them to see the differences in a wrong way. Racial differences or so-called racial characteristics are only minor variations among the people groups. Scientists have found that if one were to take any two people from anywhere in the world, the basic genetic differences between these two people would typically be around 0.2%—even if they came from the same people group. But, these so-called "racial characteristics" that many think are major differences (skin color, eye shape, etc.) account for only 6% of this 0.2% variation, which amounts to a mere 0.012% difference genetically. In other words, these so-called 'racial differences' are absolutely trivial. Overall, there is more variation within any group than there is between one group and another. If a white person is looking for a tissue match for organ transplant, for instance, the best match may come from a black person and vice versa. The main reason many people think these differences are major is because they've been brought up in a culture that has taught them to see the differences this way. A scientist at the American Association for the Advancement of Science (AAAS) convention in Atlanta in 1997 stated: Race is a social construct derived mainly from the perceptions conditioned by the events of recorded history, and it has no basic biological reality.... curiously enough the idea comes very close to being of American manufacture."[103]

The Bible does not even use the word race in reference to people, but it does describe all human beings as of one blood (Acts 17:26)."[104] Oh how the enemy tries to keep these facts hidden! When we come to Christ, we become a part of His body regardless of our culture or our race. This new birth actually supersedes our culture and race. "Those who are in Christ can set aside their differences and barriers and serve and worship together because they are the 'new humanity."[105] Curtiss Paul DeYoung confirms this terminology by stating, "The Christians in Antioch were not known for any ethnic group but were called Christians in Acts 11:26." He goes on to say, "This hybrid culture that is a unique blend of the cultures, offers space for a new shared existence. Perhaps this was what the author of Ephesians described when referring to the Jews and Gentiles becoming 'one new humanity' (2:15)."[106] This presents Christians with an incredible opportunity.

Why are we still divided? "We should consider this important thought: Sin is a mistaken identity. Prejudice abounds because men do not know who they are… Sin is missing the mark. One of the Greek words for "mark" is charagma, hence the English word character. To fall short of the mark is to fall short of the character of Christ—sin is a mistaken identity. Here lies the crux of the matter, the re-occurring theme of this entire volume. From God's perspective our identity is not measured or determined by gender, race, or nationality but our identity is completely defined in Christ."[107]

We need to renew our minds and purge our cultural teachings that oppose the Word. "In the civil rights struggle the church in essence said to our culture, 'Do as we say, not as we do.' We said to culture that it was a moral imperative to integrate our schools, workplaces, and neighborhoods while simultaneously preserving the segregation that we practice in services of worship. By refusing to embody the truth claims of the gospel that we preached to our culture, we lost our credibility."[108] Actually, even if we want unity within the cultures, we reinforce division by the way we live. Oh at times churches come together for a joint service, but after we conclude the service, we go back to the way we were and nothing changes.

Instead the multicultural church must lead the way. In using the word multicultural church "we are not calling for (1) assimilation (the blending of one culture into another, usually the majority one); (2) mere integration (being just "open" to everyone to come); or (3) syncretism (the bringing together of two or three cultures—or religions—to create a new culture/religion). The goal is not homogenizing or Anglo-Americanizing the group until the expression of Christian faith is incredibly tasteless, offending no one, and satisfying to no one. By multicultural churches we are calling for a new paradigm of church which makes intentional choices to mix, accept, represent, and manifest racial and ethnic differences, but at the same time [magnifies]… the oneness of believers in Christ."[109] This church of the new millennium can show the world how to live in unity, resolve conflict, and solve the issues of racism, elitism, and prejudice.

WHITE CHURCH/ BLACK CHURCH

This is at the root of the problem. We still have the black church here and the white church over there. There is no unity, only tolerance and acceptance. Do we really think racism has changed? "Many protestant denominations in the United States have developed antiracism initiatives and encouraged their congregations to open themselves up to a greater racial diversity. Yet the separation of the white church and a black church remains entrenched."[110] Some have said to me, "Why do you always mention the white and black issue, what about the Koreans, Spanish, Burmese, etc.?" My argument here is the root of racism in America is black and white. I have found if we will deal with that one, all the races will feel welcomed.

Once we dealt with this root issue, we began to see all nations come. This has happened in The Blended Church as well as others. Yancey in his studies says "in fact, of the multiracial churches were more likely to be white and either Latino or Asian than to be white and black."[111] This statement shows me that even in the small number of multiracial churches that now exist in America, the root problem really has not been dealt with. Fred Price agrees with my assessment in his research on racism by saying; "In America, our biggest problem with racism has been black and white issue. To get to the bottom you're going to have to look at the facts that really are not as they have been painted by the media."[112]

It may seem normal that the people and churches remain separate in America but the question is, how does God view it? We must admit there is no real unity. John Wallis writes: "Why are we so willing to allow the church to be a separate entity? White church, Black church are the words we use to describe our differing embodiments of the 'Church of Jesus Christ.' How can we call ourselves the church if we are willing to allow this type of language to be used in our self-identification?

I have experienced both Black church and White church. Neither one has a monopoly on righteousness. Neither one has the one and only version of truth. In fact, both are built upon a lie. A lie that we have been preaching since this country began. Since the slaves were introduced to White Christianity in their bondage, we have accepted something that is contrary to the very God we worship. How can our God—who is love—be willing to allow us to usurp his vision for the church?

Jesus never made any statement that would preclude race as an identifying mark for any church. White church is unable to see the truth because it is too painful to admit its complicity to the lie that has perpetuated for centuries. Black church is unwilling to let go of its ownership of the pain and suffering it has endured at the hands of a greedy and self indulgent White church. Both are to blame for the lie that has been used to build our church.

Is it, or can it be God's church, if we are the ones defining who and what it is to be because we are too afraid to break out of our boxes? White church has done innumerable harms to the Black church, and it is time that the White church accepts responsibility. It is also time for the Black church to stop relying on the pain of the past as its measuring stick for the present. It is obvious from our sordid history that the USA is built on the oppression of one group over another. Our attempt to create what the White church saw as religious utopia has resulted in a distorted and plastic rendition of what our creator envisioned. God has been patient with us for centuries, and it is time that we stop lying to ourselves about how we have created the church.

Church is to be a place where all that accept the challenge of Christ can come and be fed and in turn feed others. It is also a place where we are to worship God. What God wants the church to be a place we can all express our love and devotion to God in a way that shows how deeply God's love has changed our lives."[113]

The book *United By Faith* makes this statement about racism: "it's a stain on the churches witness."[114] The White/Black church is a clear failure of the church to the unbelievers in the United States. They hear us preach love, acceptance, and unity and then watch us segregate. My experience and research have shown that we (as the body of Christ) must first deal with the black and white issue. When we do that, then all races, tribes, and tongues will unite.

Tony Campolo is a prolific writer and a man who has led with action, not just talk. When he was dealing with the conviction of these thoughts on racism he went and joined a black church. That was a positive step but not the answer. The underlying issues still remain the same.

One experiment that may confirm my thesis was the actions of Bishop Fred A. Caldwell. Bishop Caldwell pastors a large African American congregation in Shreveport, Louisiana. He wanted to build a multicultural church, so he began to pay non-blacks five dollars an hour to set through Sunday morning services and $10 an hour to attend the church's Thursday night service. This experiment was soon picked up by the local Shreveport newspaper and in papers across the United States, including the USA Today. Reports after one year were that thousands of dollars were spent but the church was right back where it started as being predominantly African-American.

Jonathan Hartgrove and his wife (a white couple) joined a black church while they were studying at Duke University. He writes that "we could not worship the black Christ without becoming black, however, becoming black meant forsaking our white identity."[115] A statement I will make over and over is that coming together in unity does not mean we all act alike. Unity is not conformity, and as a multicultural church, it's important to celebrate our diversity! Every ethnicity has a deposit of God in it. Without us coming together we will never experience His fullness and show forth His full glory.

What must change for a predominantly white church or black church to become multicultural? Some of our traditions must be challenged. Our religious myths and twisted theology must be confronted. A willingness to change what we teach, how we do church, and to accept the pain that the changes will bring must be adopted. We will have to be willing to sacrifice and change the way we do things if we want to bring all nations in. To build a church around our personal culture and expect others to adapt is not going to work.

This is also a big issue on the mission field of foreign lands. We try at times to Americanize people instead of Christianize them. One major problem with each culture is we attempt to worship a god who looks like ourselves. We build gods who look like us and who support and emphasize our own culture. I heard Anne Lamott say: "You know that you've created God in your own image when it turns out that He hates all the same people you do." Tony Campolo took it a step further and began to question the real racial issues most were scared to discuss. He began to bring out research done by Emile Durkheim in his book "The Elementary Forms of the Religious Life," and discuss "the totem effect and how it feeds into America's preaching of a Eurocentric Jesus.[116] In a white church there hangs a picture of Jesus as white with blue eyes. Not to mention every disciple, prophet, and person the bible ever mentions is also white. It's no different than when you go into a black church and there hangs a picture of a black Jesus with an afro. Likewise, the last supper picture has thirteen black people. "The tendency of man is to cast God in the image of our own culture, to say, God is like me. There is a human need in our fallen nature to think ourselves superior to others. Every culture has the tendency to find a scapegoat, oppressively dealing with another group or individuals. If I carry into my Christianity any value I was raised with, no matter how worthy it may seem to be, I am tolerating something that puts down another group of people, then I am casting God in my own image. There are enjoyable traditions unique to each people group by reason that God put a creative capacity into the image of man. These traditions are fully desirable except to the degree that they have been tainted by sin, and moralizing or degenerating others."[117]

I have heard so many when questioned about a picture of a white or black Jesus say, "Well, I know but...." This is the problem; it does have an effect. We Christians have a lot of soul searching to do. We cannot allow culture to override our Christian values found in the Bible. We know the pain of black history, and must retain clarity that these many injustices were the result of race and color trumping Christian principles. God has called us to unity. It was Paul who shared a truth that should guide our mindset as Christians toward each other.

PHIL 2:2-4

Fulfill my joy by being like-minded, having the same love, being of one accord, of one mind. Let nothing be done through selfish ambition or conceit, but in lowliness of mind let each esteem others better than himself. Let each of you look out not only for his own interests, but also for the interests of others.

Is this our mindset? Do we really "esteem others better than ourselves?" Does the world see us Christians treating one another like this? This type of attitude would draw the lost to Christ. When they see us segregating, does it repel them?

CHALLENGING WHITE CHURCH TRADITIONS.

W hile I have already shared some things that have to change, these next few chapters will be very difficult to process for some. It's like kicking over some sacred cows and when they are attacked, or even just challenged, it brings high emotions to the table. My goal is unity, not separation. I have seen many who were challenged quit at this point, so please move ahead with prayer. We must look at some issues many have refused to discuss. This is not an attack on the white church, but a challenge to change our direction for the future of reaching the nations.

My research and experience reveal churches are still segregated because Caucasian churches generally don't know how to facilitate racial integration. "White pastors often think they have done all that is necessary when they verbally state that their churches are nondiscriminatory and that black people are welcome in their congregations. What they don't realize is that the black people who join these white churches often would be in the upper socioeconomic brackets of black congregations. In short, white churches, especially in the suburbs, are all too ready to welcome black professionals into their membership, but not the lower classes. White churches will even take a certain degree of pride in pointing out that they have black people who are in their pews without recognizing that any congregation would be thrilled to have doctors, lawyers, teachers, and other professionals in their churches, regardless of racial identity. These white churches open their doors to well-to-do African American congregants and seldom receive those who come from the underclass of the social system. Seldom do those on public welfare or with prison records show up in these mainline, upper-middle-class, white churches."[118]

A black doctor will be welcomed in a white church, but what about the uneducated? Will they be taken in and loved? Will they be invited out to lunch after service? For the most part, that answer is no! Is it a taught behavior that whites view blacks with no education or money as a lower class of human? I know that would not be spoken out loud, but what are the attitudes of the heart? We have no idea of their story, so to make a prejudgment, or to stereotype them is *sin*!

"Middle-class white people will often view the areas that are racially and ethnically diverse as having high crime rates and being ridden with drugs. These images are perpetuated by news coverage and the media in general. Coverage is only given to incidents of violence and rarely are these neighborhoods highlighted in a positive manner. Sociologically speaking, there is some truth to these perceptions because economics often produce situations where people have no other option than to risk illegal activity. But the consequence is that European Americans link violence with racial and ethnic diversity."[119]

So all white Christians must go back and challenge our process of beliefs that many times results in racism thinking. A survey of Caucasian people conducted, found that many Caucasian people "still view blacks as less hardworking and ambitious, or as more aggressive or violence prone than whites."[120] More research found that "usually only a *minority* of the residents [in low income neighborhoods] exhibit the antisocial behavior often condemned by whites as typical of black America. In most low-income neighborhoods, the majority of people hold to traditional work and family values, and still hope to succeed despite discrimination and their very difficult living environments."[121]

While the political divide between whites and blacks is a sensitive issue, discussion is merited. The inner-city neighborhoods are the hot potato at the root of the division. Even the abortion issue that most Christian whites are so easily angered over still has its root in the inner cities when discussed among the blacks. However, I would fail the church if I did not share some thoughts from David Anderson, a black pastor who has done a great deal to fight the racism in the church. Anderson has worked extensively with Bill Hybels and Willowcreek church. He felt like ultraconservative politics were pushed at him anytime he would go into a white church and/or be a speaker on a Christian program that involved white people. He states, "To redefine certain political issues as 'Christian' issues really makes true Christians who happen to be on the other side of the political spectrum question their commitment to Christ. Do you really want me to question my faith because you question my stance on non-moral issues such as bigger tax cuts? I hope not. Saddest of all is how many times I have been among white people (who assumed I was a Republican) and heard with my own ears people question how anyone could be a Christian and be a Democrat. Likewise, I have been among black people (who assumed I was a Democrat) and heard the opposite charge. How this must grieve our Lord Jesus, who was, contrary to popular belief, neither a Democrat nor a Republican!"[122]

Other sacred cows for the white church rests in statements listed below;

"People want to worship with their own kind."

"We live in a white neighborhood."

"The church has always been this way."

Do we use these excuses to justify having segregated churches? Yes, I said *excuses,* and I understand this may have angered you, but I have to challenge ideas and thoughts we have allowed to slip by. Jack Hayford believes that the church remaining passive during such times as the Civil Rights Movement was detrimental to racial relations. He said, "I did not realize how blinded I was in my attitude toward the civil rights movement of the 1960s. By that time, I was working in the headquarters of our denominational offices. I was passive toward what was taking place in the black community that was seeking to establish its civil rights; I did not realize how that passivity was being read by my evangelical brothers and sisters in the black community."[123] The church must stop remaining passive. When injustices such as racism infiltrate the church, we must become proactive and take a stand. Remaining passive is one of the vehicles that is used by the author of lies and division.[124]

During the research conducted by Feagin and O'Brien, they found that, "More or less stereotyped understandings often creep into white attitudes, assessments, and commentaries about African Americans, and stereotyped understandings can under gird even apparently nonracial analyses of group differences and related social matters."[125] The white church has several characteristics that classify it as such. One of them is that its function is to sustain the power of the dominant group, in this case, the white group. Another characteristic is that the power is centralized among a small group of long time members. This dominant group "clings to irrational thoughts, made rational in their minds, in order to justify hoarding their power. Because they may feel powerless in other relationships in their lives, which is often the psychological reason that people hoard power in churches, their self-esteem rests upon their ability to sustain that power."[126] Remember I discussed earlier the breakthrough that happens when a church has multiple races represented on staff. Kivel believes it is important to assess the culture of power. He believes this will recognize the white culture of power so that it can be challenged and dealt with. He suggests this be done by asking a series of questions.

Is there a white culture of power, and if so, what does it look like—

In your office or area where you work?

In your school or classroom?

In your living room or living space?

In your congregation?

Where you go out to eat?

Where you shop for clothes?

In agencies whose services you use?

Some questions you might ask yourself to identify the culture of power and its appearance include:

Who is in authority?

How is the space designed?

What is on the walls?

What language(s) are used? Which are acceptable?

What music and food is available?

Who has credibility?

Who is treated with full respect?

Whose experience is valued?

Whose voices are heard?

Who decides?[127]

Being truthful in the responses to these questions can help determine some of the attitudes and beliefs that have formed the traditions in a church. It also helps give insight into the influences of a church, and those influences can therefore, be changed to be more accommodating to the different cultures and races of a church.

One of my major issues with the white church has been the pushing off of the responsibility of taking the first step. I strongly feel that since the white church has not suffered the effects of racism, as the black church, it should be the first to move into action to fix it. "The white church has done innumerable harms to the black church, and it is time that the white church accepts responsibility."[128] The white church has committed many sins towards African Americans and has in turn helped to perpetuate racist attitudes that still exist today. It is important that the white church accepts responsibility, asks for forgiveness, and is willing to move towards reconciliation. Hayford issues this challenge to churches, "If we are going to model to the world that Jesus raised up the church to be unified (in contrast to the world in its separatism), and if we are going to penetrate the urban centers of the world (nearly all of which are a melting together of races), then we are going to have to learn to overcome some of the encrusted points of separation in our system. These are not always points of bitter resistance, but unperceived points of separation that encrust themselves in our souls. Let us do something about it. This begins on a personal level."[129]

CHAPTER TWELVE

THE WHITE CHURCH TEACHING OF TWISTED THEOLOGY AND RELIGIOUS MYTHS.

Over the years of dealing with racism in the church, the lack of biblical understanding among white people on blacks in the bible is astounding. Since most whites ignore the issue of racism, it probably explains the lack of study on the issue. Are there blacks in the Bible? Why are there different races and where did they come from? Are we to remain separated and what about multiracial marriages? Where do the stories come from that say black people are cursed? The myths and ignorance that are common among white Christians are astounding and reasons racism flourishes in the church.

Men like Cyrus Ingerson Scofield,[130] and Finnis Dake,[131] have perpetuated the poison of racism and separation. These men did some good things for Christianity but made huge errors in their writing concerning racism. The Dake's Bible lists 39 reasons why the races should be segregated. It's clearly racist propaganda. Unfortunately, it's been preached from the pulpit and influenced thousands of lives. "Dake's impact upon conservative Pentecostalism cannot be over-stated. Between 1961 and 1988 372,000 volumes of his Bible had rolled off the presses, and an estimated 28,000 to 30,000 were still being sold annually."[132] I must add the company did print a new bible in January of 1997 that omitted the racist remarks. However, the damage has been done.

The Scofield Bible that was first published in 1909 and then revised in 1917 has done even more damage in the area of racism. Former Dallas theological seminary president and student of Scofield's theology John F. Walvoord commented on this reference Bible by saying: "this edition of the Bible which has had an unprecedented circulation, has popular-ized pre-millennial teachings (and others, including racism) and provided ready helps of interpretation. It has probably done more to extend premillennialism in the last half century than any other volume... This accounts for the many attempts to discredit his work... However, the Bible continues to be re-issued year after year in greater numbers than any of its refuters."[133] John's comments here were not focused on the racism issue, but I want to share this mater-ial's influence throughout the country. So let's look at Scoffield's comments that have tied into and supported a twisted racist theology preached from white pulpits and universities. The basis of the lie starts with his interpretation of the following scripture:

GENESIS 9:18- 29 (NKJV)

Now the sons of Noah who went out of the ark were Shem, Ham, and Japheth. And Ham was the father of Canaan. These three were the sons of Noah, and from these the whole earth was populated. And Noah began to be a farmer, and he planted a vineyard. Then he drank of the wine and was drunk, and became uncovered in his tent. And Ham, the father of Canaan, saw the nakedness of his father, and told his two brothers outside. But Shem and Japheth took a garment, laid it on both their shoulders, and went backward and covered the nakedness of their father. Their faces were turned away, and they did not see their father's nakedness. So Noah awoke from his wine, and knew what his younger son had done to him. Then he said: "Cursed be Canaan; A servant of servants He shall be to his brethren." And he said: "Blessed be the LORD, The God of Shem, And may Canaan be his servant. May God enlarge Japheth, And may he dwell in the tents of Shem; And may Canaan be his servant." And Noah lived after the flood three hundred and fifty years. So all the days of Noah were nine hundred and fifty years; and he died.

Scofield says in his notes commenting on the above passage, "a prophetic declaration is made that from Ham will descend an inferior and servile posterity.[134] Excuse me! That is not what it said. Ham was not cursed, Canaan was. Ham was blessed and I will show you from the scripture. Furthermore, where did he find the word *inferior*? I don't see that, do you?

There is a movie that is based on a true story called Mississippi Burning. A comment was made in the movie which was taken from FBI files, and I want you to hear what was said. This was a statement made by the deputy's wife, "you don't understand, you don't understand. Racism is what I've grown up with. I was taught in school since third grade. They said that it said it in the Bible. Genesis 9:27 when God said, "May God enlarge Japheth, and may he dwell in the tents of Shem, and may Canaan be his servant." She kept saying, "This is what we've learned. This is what we've been taught."[135] Yes, this is the fruit of a twisted theology.

So let's break down the scripture and get it straight. Gen 9:27:

May God enlarge Japheth, and may he dwell in the tents of Shem, and may Canaan be his servant.

Japheth is one of the sons of Noah. Canaan was not Noah's son. Canaan was Noah's grandson.

GENESIS 9:1:

So God blessed Noah and the sons.

God blessed Noah and his sons. Noah had three sons. Their names are Shem, Ham, and Japheth.

GENESIS 9:18-24

Now the sons of Noah who went out of the ark were Shem, Ham, and Japheth. And Ham was the father of Canaan. These three were the sons of Noah, and from these the whole earth was populated. And Noah began to be a farmer, and he planted a vineyard. Then he drank of the wine and was drunk, and became uncovered in his tent. And Ham, the father of Canaan, saw the nakedness of his father, and told his two brothers outside. But Shem and Japheth took a garment, laid it on both their shoulders, and went backward and covered the nakedness of their father. Their faces were turned away, and they did not see their father's nakedness. So Noah awoke from his wine, and knew what his younger son had done to him.

There are a few things to notice. The sons are Shem, Ham and Japheth. Where is Ham in the chronological order here? He's second. Everything the Bible says, every detail has significance. Noah had three sons and the middle son was Ham. Ham actually had four children. Why are we not told about the other children? Why didn't he tell us who Shem's sons or Japheth's sons were? Furthermore, there is significance that he tells us about Canaan. That's why only about one grandchild out of all the grandchildren was mentioned. There was a problem with Canaan and that's the reason it's mentioned and brought out here. "These three were the sons of Noah and from these three the whole earth was populated.

The name Ham basically means dark or burnt. And through historical genealogy lines, we trace back that Ham was the father of the darker skinned people. Notice the Bible doesn't say Ham was cursed. Shem was dusty or olive colored. And Japheth means bright or fair, but he still had color in him. He was a lighter complexion. From tracing the biblical table of nations, (See Genesis 10), we can see that Ham is considered to be the father of the blacks, the Mongoloids, the Indians. Shem is the father to the Semites, the Jewish, the Arabic. Japheth was the father of the Caucasians. William DeWhite McKissick Sr's book, Beyond Roots: In Search Of Blacks In The Bible, is a classic when it comes to tracing the roots of blacks in the Bible. His teaching on the ethnicity of Ham is both scholarly and profound. He also proves his teaching not only from a biblical standpoint but with doctors and anthropologist agreeing with his findings.[136]

GENESIS 10:6

The sons of Ham were Cush, Mizraim, Put, and Canaan.

Now we've heard Canaan mentioned twice, but we haven't heard mention of the other children. We can trace back through biblical genealogies that Cush was Ethiopian; Mizraim was Egyptian; Put was Libyan; and Canaan was Palestinian. Who ruled the world for years with great power like the United States has in our time? Egypt, at one time, was a great power on the earth. We can trace Egyptians back to Ham. They were people of color. So the racist lies that say white people are meant to rule over black people are greatly mistaken. Amazing things happened in Egypt. Where did the pyramids come from? We still can't figure it out. And it is one of the wonders of the world. Another great civilization that lived was Babylon. We can trace that through Ham also. They ruled for around 2,000 years. Then the time came when Shem's family was in power. That was the time of the crusades, of the Arabs, and the Jewish people. Now we see the times of Japheth ruling. Those who say that white people are smarter or better are absolutely foolish. The histories of the past civilizations prove that wrong.

Let's go back to the curse of Canaan. If Ham his father was cursed why was he not black as the racists teach? Let me explain it better by looking in detail at Gen 9.

GEN 9:22

"Ham the father of Canaan saw the nakedness of his father."

That is a key verse.

"He became uncovered in his tent and Ham the father of Canaan saw the nakedness of his father and told his two brothers outside. But Shem and Japheth both took the garment laid it on their shoulders and covered the nakedness of their father. Their faces were turned away. They did not see their father's nakedness. Now Noah awoke from his wine and knew what *his younger son* had done to him."

His Younger son it says? I thought Ham was the second son? When we see the word son, many times it does not refer to the direct son. It may be a grandson or great grandson. The scripture reveals it. For example, the bible says that Jesus was the son of David. We know there were many generations between them. The Bible says the Jews are the sons of Abraham. Here too, there are many generations. So, here, it's talking about lineage, not a direct son. If we just say the younger son it cannot mean Ham because Ham was the second son, not the youngest. However, Canaan was the youngest son of Ham.

GEN 9:24

So Noah awoke from his wine and knew what his younger son had done to him.

If Ham only looked at him and that was the sin, how would Noah have known being he was drunk and asleep? However, if someone violated you, when you woke up you would know that. Noah knew something had happened to him. He had been violated. It could not have been that Ham was just looking.

GEN 9:25

Then he said: cursed be Canaan.

However, many have been taught that blacks came from the curse. The racist lies have said God cursed Ham's family and they all became black. They teach it in their theology as the curse of Ham. However, that is not what the Bible says. It does not say that they turned black. Canaan was cursed not Ham. The good news is black people are not cursed. However, even a greater truth comes out when investigated even further.

Luther Blackwell's comments on this passage have been enlightening to many. "How many times have you read this verse and it seemed straight forward, doesn't it? Look close, the Bible said Noah knew what his youngest son had done to him. Ham was the second son.

I recruited some specialized help, and asked the opinion of the respected Jewish rabbi on the east coast who is a recognized expert in ancient Hebrew and Hebraic idioms. Idioms are a term of speech that are not meant to be literal descriptions. The English idiom, he's the baby of the family, can apply to a 50-year-old father of three kids if he was the youngest of the parents. This rabbi confirmed my suspicions. When verse 24 says youngest son, it is using a Jewish idiom which is still in use today. That idiom, (beno haqqeton), means 'the smallest son,' and it is highly likely that it is an idiom for grandson. That solves the first problem.

Secondly in verse 24 it says Noah knew what his youngest son had done to him. Now if somebody just looks at me while I'm sleeping, there's no way I'd know about it unless someone told me. The Bible only tells us two of Noah sons covered his nakedness, well evidently he was still asleep.

What ever happened, Noah knew it had happened when he woke up without any one else's help.

Once again, the rabbi brought the light of ancient rabbinical thought to the problem. In verse 22 the Hebrew word for nakedness here is (Ervah). This word nearly always implies more than mere looking. And Noah awoke and he knew what had been done to him, and who had done it. We have to conclude that the lewd sexual act took place when Noah was half asleep or groggy. And when his senses returned his temper flared and he went after Canaan not Ham.

Our rabbinical source says the Hebrew word translated *saw* in verse 22 carries much more meaning than the English translation implies. The Hebrew word is (raah), while the root is (ra) which in every case has the connotation of evil. So (raah) means evil looking, looking with a lustful eye, for licentious purpose. It also carries the meaning of excitement joyful enjoyment, prolonged staring or spying, and approval. Now we have both the words solved in the word nakedness doubling the sense of evil intent and purpose and this verse.

Ham just didn't trot out to his brothers and say 'I accidentally saw something terrible a moment ago and we need to help our poor old dad.' No, I get the feeling that he ran to Shem and Japheth with excitement. 'Our dad, you know our holy dad, the one who kept us under his thumb, the one who said there are certain things that you are going to do in my house and other things that you're not going to do. You ought to see what he and Canaan are doing right now. I can hardly keep from laughing.'

The Bible clearly implies that Ham enjoyed what ever he saw going on in that tent. He enjoyed watching the nakedness and vulnerability of his drunken father."[137]

So think about this first, who lets a drunken man put curses on people, and the curse lives forever? Was Noah not drunk? You think God is going to honor when Noah said: "cursed be Canaan." People say a lot of bad things when they're drunk. Thank God He didn't honor that. It was not God that cursed him, it was Noah. The curse was upon Canaan and his decendants. Regardless, the curse was fulfilled biblically when the Jewish people conquered over the Canaanites. If there was a curse that God allowed it had to be that. Tony Evans says: "Never mind that the bible placed limitations on curses for up to three or four generations (Exodus 20:5). Never mind that the curse on Canaan and his descendants finds it's most obvious fulfillment in the ongoing defeat and subjugation of Canaan by Israel (Joshua 9:23; 1 Kings 9:20-21). Never mind that only one of Ham's sons were cursed and not all four. Therefore, all black people everywhere could not be cursed."[138] It said Canaan shall serve Japheth and Shem. However, the question is, when? We know for 4,000 years that never happened. I believe that prophecy has already been fulfilled. However, regardless of what it is, it says nowhere they became black because of the curse.

If we are going to talk about curses, let's get biblical. I know two places in the Bible where God cursed people and they both involved leprosy. In Numbers 12, Moses married an Ethiopian woman. Ethiopian women are usually black. Some are saying, you mean Moses married a black woman? Yes he did. It is so evident that Aaron and his sister Miriam got mad because he married her, a woman of another race. The interracial marriage they did not approve of.

NUMBERS 12:1

Then Miriam and Aaron spoke against Moses because of the Ethiopian woman whom he had married; for he had married an Ethiopian woman.

Next look what God said about the comments of Miriam and Aaron.

NUMBERS 12:9-10

So the anger of the LORD was aroused against them, and He departed. And when the cloud departed from above the tabernacle, suddenly Miriam became leprous, as white as snow. Then Aaron turned toward Miriam, and there she was, a leper.

So if you are going to talk about a curse (I'm not saying the white people are cursed) when God cursed her, she became white, not black.

2 KINGS 5:27

Therefore the leprosy of Naaman shall cling to you and your descendants forever." And he went out from his presence leprous, as white as snow.

If God cursed Ham's son for what Ham did, would this not be wrong? Why did God not curse the other sons of Ham? Why did Canaan take the heat? If God really honored the curse that Noah put on Canaan, why did Ham become black, and what about his other brothers? They didn't have anything to do with it. Thank God I haven't been punished for my brother's sins. I have enough problems with my own. So the idea that the black people are black because of the curse is absolutely misconstrued.

Even as late as 1994 we see this myth that blacks are inferior spreading. Tee Garlington writes that: "Racism is as old as recorded history itself, and it is as current as today's newspaper. In the 1994 book the Bell Curve, Charles Murray and Richard Herrnstein present an academic argument on an old theme. Their premise is that certain people are more intelligent or less intelligent than other people based solely on the race to which they have been classified."[139] This book was written by professors from Harvard but filled with statistics, graphs, and old myths. Chapters thirteen and fourteen brings out that blacks have a lower IQ or intelligence than whites.[140] This book not only paints a picture of race superiority but also criminal and evil inheritance. In one of many books that followed, Steven Fraser suggests, "that The Bell Curve's claim to offer scientific proof of the inferiority of black people was bound to eclipse all its other possible subjects in public debate." He goes on to say, "the book colors the class structure in unmistakable shades of black and white."[141]

We as Christians base our beliefs and views on the Word regardless of science. The Word stands on solid ground while men's understanding of science changes constantly. For example, a Newsweek article in 1995 reveals that: scientists are now questioning the validity of race as a basis of classifying human beings. In a 1989 scientific survey, 70 percent of the cultural anthropologists rejected race as a biological category. Currently, scientists are considering the possibility that research involving genes and chromosomes may become a more valid way to classify groups of people."[142]

Chapter Thirteen -Challenging Black Church Traditions.

This chapter is not an attack on the black church. The black church lived through very difficult times and was the backbone to bring oppressed people to freedom. However, two items have held the movement back, brought confusion to its perception, and kept it obscure or unintegrated. One is the perpetual traditions that were birthed because of slavery but are practiced today. The other item is the stance of the black church that has been conservative in theology and liberal in social issues. In these last days, the black church has to move to post black church traditions. I participated on a panel of pastors in a conference discussing the issues of racism. The floor had been opened up for questions on how to fix racism in the church. I had been asked a question and finished answering, when an outburst happened. A black pastor stood up, the material from his lap flying all over the place (not sure if he threw it or out of being so emotional he forgot about it), and began to shout, "You white pastors who claim to be building multicultural churches take our black people from us, but never send any whites to our church." The air which was filled with peace soon over-flowed with tension as all eyes were fixed on me. Without much time to think I heard myself ask, "what time do your services start?" Not sure what was really being asked of him, he said, "Ten a.m." My next question was, "So what time do you really start?" Around eleven am, he exclaimed. Well, I said, even if I sent them to you, they would never stay, for when you say it starts at ten, that's what they expect. He is a wonderful man of God but was so steeped in his tradition that he never gave it a brief thought how other cultures felt about the time issue. This issue is one of the traditions of the black church that were developed from the days of slavery, but that now seems natural. They are keeping the black church exclusive.

"African American congregations were places where political and social leadership developed and the interests of the black community were furthered. African American congregations were the cultural womb of the black commu-nity, giving birth too many of the vital institutions within the African American community such as schools, banks, insur-ance companies, and low-income housing."[143] Craig Van

Gelder adds, "The African American church served as the hub of a parallel community within broader white society."[144]

Beginning in the 1700s, increasing numbers of slaves converted to religions such as the Methodist and Baptist faiths. Members of these denominations promoted the biblical idea that all Christians were equal in the sight of God. This provided hope to the slaves. The churches also encouraged worship in ways that many Africans found to be similar to African worship patterns, with enthusiastic singing, clapping, and dancing. Many Caucasian slave owners, however, preached strict obedience and required attendance at Caucasian churches. The owners were fearful that the slaves would rebel if they were allowed to worship on their own. The hypocrisy of the church was evident to many slaves, since they believed the Christian message that they were all equal in God's view.[145]

In the slave quarters, however, African Americans created their own church. Through signals, passwords, and messages, they called believers to services where they freely mixed African rhythms, singing, and beliefs with evangelical Christianity. These spirituals, with their double meanings of eternal salvation and freedom from slavery, were developed. Black preachers perfected their intoned style of extemporaneous preaching. Part church, part psychological refuge, and part organizing point for occasional acts of outright rebellion, these meetings provided a way for enslaved African Americans to express and enact their hopes for a better future.[146] This became the birthing place of the Black church.

According to the research done by Tony Campolo and Michael Battle, the modern black church can be generalized into three categories. They are the storefront church, the black mega church, and the denominational mainline church.[147] In order to understand the black church, how it is structured, and why it is designed that way, it is important to understand these three types of churches.

The storefront church is one where the pastor is generally a self-appointed clergyman, with little or no formal seminary education, who has attracted a small congregation of people, generally no more than fifty. Many of these pastors have another job besides being a pastor in order to earn a living. Storefront churches are generally found in poor neighborhoods and urban areas. Worship at these churches tends to be emotional. Generally black gospel songs are performed. Prosperity theology is often preached with an emphasis on tithing. There is also much emphasis on miracles that God performs for those who are faithful. Storefront churches have provided a strong foundation for people to develop in their discipleship to Christ. However, these churches are often looked down upon or even completely ignored by both black and Caucasian churches that surround them.[148]

The black mega churches are generally independent of denomination affiliations. However, they tend to draw heavily from Pentecostalism. Like the storefront churches, healing ministries are generally a significant part of the church. The Worship at the mega churches is usually broadcasted via radio, television, and now, even the internet. The key component to a black mega church is the pastor and his preaching that is done there. Oftentimes, "Their churches are so much a product of dynamism of their preaching that people commonly regard the church by the name of the pastor and often forget that the church itself has a name."[149] Many black mega churches have a vast array of resources and outreach programs to the local communities they serve. This is one reason why they are so important to the black community. However, mega churches generally do not work with other churches in their area, thus, making it more difficult to build bridges between different communities.

Mainline denominational churches usually range in size from a few hundred to a few thousand congregants. Pastors of these churches are normally college educated in addition to going through seminary school.[150]

So let us now consider some of the traditions that are carried from one generation to the next that cause the black church isolation. The one aforementioned is that of time. It is frustrating to many when services start later than they are supposed to and when people arrive late. Punctuality is an important trait to many people. This is one reason that Caucasian people do not feel comfortable attending a black church. Kim Gordon asks, "Why do so many of us [black Americans] show up late in an almost consistent, predictable way?" Is it a genetically coded, innate trait, a lack of discipline, or a stubborn refusal to give Time a monopoly over our lives? Are we unwilling to go along for the ride with a fast-paced, alarm clock-oriented world, or are we valiantly holding onto cultural and spiritual traditions that served our ancestors for thousands of years?[151]

Gordon goes on to say, "The deep-seated resentment of attempts to control all phases of their [slaves] lives through the clock, coupled with a natural, cyclical, task-oriented mindset, led to a form of resistance that often refuses to adhere to a strict, minutely-dissected definition of time. That phenomenon has come to be called Colored People's Time."[152] In the days of slavery church was about the only place the black people could go and be free to do it as they pleased. So Sunday became the day of freedom and was a whole day experience. So getting there at an exact time in the morning was not an issue. That thought has been passed down and accepted. The problem is it's now hindering growth and keeping whites from coming, or staying if they do come. This has to be addressed immediately if the African-American church wants to attract a more multicultural population.

The length of service is also an issue that will cause white people to not attend and join a black congregation. In the days of slavery the church was a day of community fellowship and was an all day Sunday event. Those days are past and three hour services are too long for most church attendees. Services can be shortened, and done in order without lasting all day. Some have said "we don't want to grieve the Holy Spirit." This can be done with out grieving the Holy Spirit.

Much research has shown we can shorten our singing time and preaching time. The attention span of people has shortened significantly and people check out mentally if we continue to long. I once heard a man say "preachers think they are better than they really are, and the proof rest in the fact that they go on and on."

With today's technology, we can utilize our time more effective. A few ideas one may consider are; putting scripture up on screens, this saves wasted time while everyone searches for the verse in their bible. Announcements can be done on video, this is more effective due to our media driven society and saves time from someone fumbling through the reading. Using the video announcements saves people coming up front, leaving the stage or altar area and sitting down, introductions, and greatly reduces people getting off track while talking. Testimonies are also effective on video and cut down the transition time. Our web site has some video ideas to help you, software that can be used and is cost effective.

What We Wear To Church

Dressing up in an ornate fashion with your best clothes and woman wearing big hats is another issue. Dressing up in itself is not the issue. The issue comes into effect when everyone has to dress up to be accepted, loved or respected. Sundays were the only day most blacks could wear good clothes so that's why they did it. It was also a sign of freedom and prosperity under such bondage in modern times. This is not always comfortable for people who prefer to be comfortable, or who cannot afford such outfits. "When they were forbidden because of prejudice to enter public gathering places, African-Americans isolated themselves to avoid conflict with prejudiced persons. This isolation could have been disastrous to their personalities. To restore their self-dignity, they wore beautiful clothes symbolizing their inner worth. Their churches were places where they could wear stunning clothes, so dressing for the Lord had two purposes."[153]

The pastors generally wear robes during service, and in public are dressed in suits. Members of the congregation will come to church dressed in their finest apparel. Dressing in casual clothes is looked down upon.[154] A visitor to an African-American church can feel underdressed because of the elaborate clothing. It has even caused competition among believers. This is a church tradition that could be difficult for younger church-goers to embrace. In order to attract a more diverse crowd, a less elaborate dress code should be embraced. These are all issues that the black church must look at in order to become more multicultural.

Another obstacle is the treating of a black pastor as a king, while he lives above the congregation's lifestyle. All pastors should be honored, but he must live among the congregation within their means.

1 PETER 5:1-3

The elders who are among you I exhort, I who am a fellow elder and a witness of the sufferings of Christ, and also a partaker of the glory that will be revealed: Shepherd the flock of God which is among you, serving as overseers, not by compulsion but willingly, not for dishonest gain but eagerly; nor as being lords over those entrusted to you, but being examples to the flock;

In the days of slavery, the pastor was often times the only black man allowed to read, get an education, talk among the whites or be among the whites. The black pastor was the only free voice to speak and empower the people. He was the only political voice for oppressed people. So he became the representation of the whole black community and was so revered. However, today anyone can succeed in this society if an effort is made. As pastors in this day and age, we must live among the people, not above them. This privilege has become a stumbling block to many unbelievers that have seen the abuse and excess portrayed by clergy members. By reading the Bible one can see that Jesus was among the people while the Pharisees lived above the people. The pastor must be able to identify with his congregation. The black pastor was and has been a voice to stand for social justice. The last decade shifted as many pastors began to preach a gospel that encourages them to drive the best vehicles, wear the best clothes, and jewelry. This has been a great turn off for unbelievers that are living below the poverty level. Let me make it clear that this doctrinal issue has also affected many white pastors and white churches.

Another major cause of division of the white church/black church is an underlying infectious thought of an anti-white victim-hood mindset. This causes the white people who want to unify to stand back and say, that this is a divide that they can not or do not know how to cross. Many whites have acknowledged the terrible racism that has occurred, but need to be helped or coached on how to unify now. When black leaders cry out that the government created AIDS in order to kill off minorities, or the problem with the world is it is run by rich white people, this only widens the divide. The teaching and thought of black leaders who say, "we are victims and our recourse is to blame," only isolates. The isolation leads to anger, resentment, unforgivingness, and the like. A result of some of this thought has caused some of the younger blacks to focus on the negative and the anger. They lose focus on the positive concept that through hard work they can overcome and excel. I agree it's harder for the young black male than young white male, to excel, so they need to be taught to use the negative as a motivation factor. Anger, blame, isolation, resentment, hatred, and a victim mentality is not birthed by the Spirit of Christ.

GALATIANS 5:13-26

For you, brethren, have been called to liberty; only do not use liberty as an opportunity for the flesh, but through love serve one another. For all the law is fulfilled in one word, even in this: "You shall love your neighbor as yourself. But if you bite and devour one another, beware lest you be consumed by one another! I say then: Walk in the Spirit, and you shall not fulfill the lust of the flesh. For the flesh lusts against the Spirit, and the Spirit against the flesh; and these are contrary to one another, so that you do not do the things that you wish. But if you are led by the Spirit, you are not under the law.

Now the works of the flesh are evident, which are: adultery, fornication, uncleanness, lewdness, idolatry, sorcery, hatred, contentions, jealousies, outbursts of wrath, selfish ambitions, dissensions, heresies, envy, murders, drunkenness, revelries, and the like; of which I tell you beforehand, just as I also told you in time past, that those who practice such things will not inherit the kingdom of God. But the fruit of the Spirit is love, joy, peace, longsuffering, kindness, goodness, faithfulness, gentleness, self-control. Against such there is no law. And those who are Christ's have crucified the flesh with its passions and desires. If we live in the Spirit, let us also walk in the Spirit. Let us not become conceited, provoking one another, envying one another.

When God delivered the children of Israel out of the hand of the Egyptians he had them wander the wilderness to attempt to get the slave mentality out of them. Even though delivered, they continued to act like a slave. In the wilderness they continually blamed, murmured, and played the victim role. The result was many never entered into the Promised Land. It is imperative that the black church doesn't cripple the next generation because of past racism and hurt. The younger generation must know the white church is not the cause of all problems that are currently facing the black community, but some of those wounds are self-inflicted. To say that the white church or white America is still the cause of all the blacks' issues is implying that blacks are still slaves and under the control of the white church or man. This victim mentality has led to some teaching black liberation theology.

CHAPTER FOURTEEN

THE BLACK CHURCH TEACHING OF BLACK LIBERATION THEOLOGY.

Black Theology was first brought out by Dr James Cone. His focus is on black power and for blacks to reject Eurocentric culture, since it is built on institutions of black slavery and suffering. DeYoung says, "Cone does not reject the biblical call for reconciliation with whites as would black separatist groups like the Nation of Islam. What he asked is that whites fully identify with oppressed African Americans and stand against white oppressors."[155] At first thought this statement seems acceptable. However, I must argue that although Cone may say he's not opposed to reconciliation, I think he is so extreme in his thought of black power that reconciliation could never happen under his theology. Cone says in his most popular book, *A Black Theology of Liberation,* that "black theology refuses to accept a God who is not identified totally with the goals of the black community." The task of Black theology is to oppose gods who do not belong to the black community."[156]

This is extreme black-power philosophy and opposed to the unity in which Jesus prayed. Is God really against all white people? J. Deotis Roberts a contemporary with Cone says, "the Christian understanding of God must develop out of the black presence in a white racist society, and out of an experience and oppression endured for almost four centuries."[157] This theology is twisted to form with black power. Of course God identifies with the struggle the blacks have had to endure under the Eurocentric church mindset, but to say He is opposed to the whites is to misrepresent His love for all mankind.

Anthony B Pinn, in his research of the black church in the post-civil-rights era says, "Cone was influenced by a speech that Bishop Henry McNeal Turner of the AME Church gave when he said 'God is in a Negro'. Cone continued this line of reasoning by claiming that the blackness of God is the essence of biblical revelation."[158] "Cone vividly vocalizes that Jesus is black: The 'raceless' American Christ has a light skin, wavy brown hair, and sometimes—wonder of wonders—blue eyes. For whites to find him with big lips and kinky hair is as offensive as it was for the Pharisees to find him partying with tax-collectors. But whether whites want to hear it or not, Christ is black, baby, with all of the features which are so detestable to white society."[159] This erroneous theology isolates the church, and we must realize

Jesus was a Jew. Ethnically, Jesus was from the Semitic line (Luke 3:23-38).

LUKE 3:23, 36

23 Now Jesus Himself began His ministry at about thirty years of age, being (as was supposed) the son of Joseph, the son of Heli,36 the son of Cainan, the son of Arphaxad, the son of Shem, the son of Noah, the son of Lamech,

The descendants of Shem are usually dusky or olive colored. Shem[160] is considered to be the ancestral father of the Semites, who are Jewish and Arabic, based on the historical and biblical research from Genesis 10 (usually referred to as the table of nations).

Christ was a Jew but clearly he had a mixture of races in His blood line, as we all do! This will be discussed in greater detail in the next chapter. Anne Lamott's quote bears repeating here: "You know that you've created God in your own image when it turns out that He hates all the same people you do." George Bernard Shaw was quoted as saying, "God created us in His image, and we decided to return the favor." We have to stop the nonsense of lowering God to our own segregated ideas and using the church pulpit to preach it from. It has not worked and will never work. The church must rise to the call in Christ that says:

GALATIANS 3:28

There is neither Jew nor Greek, slave nor free, male nor female, for you are all one in Christ Jesus.

Campolo supports my view by saying, "if we want the church to be free it would be wise not to repeat the same mistakes of our past. One way to do that would be to listen to James Cone, who is embarrassing to the church."[161] This theology of black power keeps the church divided. It perpetuates the hurts and the pains in the black church and keeps the focus on the negative. It also perpetuates thoughts for the white church of fear, separation, and hopelessness. In addition it stirs up anger which leads to further separation.

One tragic organization that fed off of the Black theology movement was the Nation of Islam. As blasphemous as the Ku Klux Klan is, it is paralleled by the Nation of Islam. Elijah Muhammad started by preaching black power and the lies against scripture. It grew worse with his followers Malcolm X. and then Louis Farrakhan. James Cone quotes Malcolm in one of his books saying" brothers and sisters, the white man has brainwashed us black people to fasten our gaze upon a blonde haired, blue-eyed Jesus! We should suffer while this white man has his milk and honey in the streets paved with gold dollars here on this earth!"[162]

From there it only escalated with Louis Farrakhan[163] taking over the Nation of Islam. The nation of Islam focuses again on race and further distorts all truth. The Nation of Islam teaches that Muhammad was a black man. Facts tell us that Muhammad was born and raised in Mecca, in South East Asia, which cannot be confused with Africa. Although, skin color does not and should not be a factor in evaluating a person, nonetheless, the untruthful presentation by Muslims, that Muhammad was black to appeal to the African-American community ought to be corrected.

The African- American community is entitled to know the truth that Muhammad was not black, rather white. There is evidence in the Hadeith (In Islamic authority, second to none but the Qur'an) that proves Muhammad was actually fair skinned. In the Islamic Hadeith Sahih El Bukhary, we read "while we were sitting with the prophet, a man came and said, 'who among you is Muhammad?' We replied, 'this white man reclining on his arm...'" (1:63). Sahih El Bukhary also refers to Muhammad as a "white person" (2:122). The Hadeith also records that when Muhammad raised his arms, "the whiteness of his armpits became visible" (2:141). These Hadeith references indicate that Muhammad was not black, rather fair skinned.

In his million Man March on Washington, DC, he had hundreds of thousands of Christians standing with him and cheering him on. I personally have on DVD and a few video tapes where Farrakhan calls himself Jesus. One is a video-tape of the April 3, 1994 Easter's message Louis Farrakhan delivered at Mosque Maryam, Chicago, Illinois, entitled, *The Crucifixion of Jesus: The Imprisonment of Minister Farrakhan.* "He (Farrakhan) discusses the crucifixion and relates it to himself, saying, 'I am hanging on the cross right now... and by my stripes you are healed. You don't have to look for Jesus. I represent him. I was born to die for you, and I love the thought of dying for you...Jesus was not born in Bethlehem but Sandersville, Georgia.'"[164] Their message is one of Black power and separation from the "White Devils." Because of angered racism they have strayed from their Christianity. A bible based church with a blend of ethnicity has the potential to penetrate these errors and affect many lives who have been sidetracked.

"He will build His church and the gates of hell shall not prevail."

CHAPTER FIFTEEN

MULTI RACIAL MARRIAGES.

This chapter is not out of place. The world is changing and the church must be able to answer the questions the world has on interracial marriage. Contrary to what some have said, these marriages are not prohibited in the Scriptures. "Often they will argue that marriage with foreigners (implying people both of different culture and color) was prohibited throughout the Old Testament. Actually, the prohibitions were not strictly against Jewish-Gentile marriages as a racial mixture, but against believer-unbeliever marriages. (Deuteronomy 7)"[165] However, the reason for this was not racial, rather, it was religious. The reason God commanded against interracial marriage was that people of other races were idolaters and worshippers of false gods. The Israelites would be led astray from God if they intermarried with idol worshippers, pagans, or heathens. A similar principle is laid out in the New Testament, but at a much different level:

2 CORINTHIANS 6:14

Do not be unequally yoked together with unbelievers. For what fellowship has righteousness with lawlessness? And what communion has light with darkness?

Just as the Israelites (believers in the one true God) were commanded not to marry idolaters, so Christians (believers in the one true God) are commanded not to marry unbelievers. To answer this question specifically, no, the Bible does not say that interracial marriage is wrong.[166] Balaam, in Numbers Chapters 25, 31 and 32, said this: here's how we can destroy the Israelites. Go in and marry their wives and introduce our gods to them, and we will destroy their nation. There are no commands or regulations to not marry a person of another race or color. There are absolutely no grounds in either the Old Testament or the New Testament to prohibit interracial marriages. Thankfully, God does not judge humans by mere external appearances. Though humans have a tendency to judge people by how they look, including their skin color, God does not judge us by color; He judges the heart. The beauty of God's judgment is that he is "no respecter of persons" (Acts 10:34), and thus we are to judge the same way (1 Timothy 5:21; James 3:17).[167] In that context, somebody asked me if I would let my daughter marry a black man. I said "I could care less about the color he is. I care more about his character and his walk with

Jesus". That is what's important to me and God! Let's talk about the reason for marriage God gives in:

MALACHI 2:15

But did He not make them one, having a remnant of the Spirit? And why one? He seeks godly offspring. Therefore take heed to your spirit, and let none deal treacherously with the wife of his youth.[168]

This is saying that God designed marriage for one reason: to produce godly offspring. That's the whole key. If you've been taught that you can't put the races together, remember we started out with one dad and mom. We've been together from the beginning. So does God support multiracial marriage? Look at these examples.

Joseph and Asneth

GENESIS 41:45

And Pharaoh called Joseph's name Zaphnath-Paaneah. And he gave him as a wife Asenath, the daughter of Poti-Pherah priest of On. So Joseph went out over all the land of Egypt.

GENESIS 41:50

And to Joseph were born two sons before the years of famine came, whom Asenath, the daughter of Poti-Pherah priest of On, bore to him.

GENESIS 41:52

And the name of the second he called Ephraim: "For God has caused me to be fruitful in the land of my affliction."

Who transcended into the land of Egypt? It was Ham and his family. So it was darker-skinned people who went there. Ephraim we trace back to Ham. (Numbers 13:8, 1 Chronicles 7:22-27) This means Joseph had a dark-skinned wife. We would call him a Jew, and he was married to what we would say today, was a black woman. Did God curse him for having a multiracial marriage? No. God blessed him. Joshua was the younger son of Asneth. So we can say that Joshua was a man of color. He was from the tribe of Ephraim (Numbers 13:8, 1 Chronicles 7:22-27). We hear people like Farrakhan say that black people aren't in the Bible. All races are represented in the scripture.

Men have created division. We have done this because the devil has tried to divide us. However, put us together and we can do something in this city, country, and world that has never been done..

Moses and Zipporah

I touched on this one in an earlier chapter but wanted to go deeper into the issue.

NUMBERS 12:1-2[169]

Then Miriam and Aaron spoke against Moses because of the Ethiopian woman whom he had married; for he had married an Ethiopian woman. So they said, "Has the LORD indeed spoken only through Moses? Has He not spoken through us also?" And the LORD heard it.

God was not displeased with Moses and Zipporah's marriage; it was the culture pressure. The Ethiopian woman was dark skinned.

NUMBERS 12:10

And when the cloud departed from above the tabernacle, suddenly Miriam became leprous, as white as snow. Then Aaron turned toward Miriam, and there she was, a leper.

Miriam, Moses sister became white as snow.

This totally contradicts the racist teaching that the black man is cursed. God cursed Miriam here and she did not turn black, but white as snow. God was not opposed to the multi racial marriage but those talking about it. Some have argued that Zipporah may not be black. Daniel Hays proves that theory is not true by saying that Cush "is used regularly to refer to the area south of Egypt, and above the cataracts on the Nile, where a Black African civilization flourished for over two thousand years. Thus it is quite clear that Moses marries a Black African woman."[170] John Piper writes "in response to Miriam's criticism, God does not get angry at Moses; he gets angry at Miriam. The criticism has to do with Moses' marriage and Moses' authority. The most explicit statement relates to the marriage: "Miriam and Aaron spoke against Moses because of the Cushite woman whom he had married, for he had married a Cushite woman." Then God strikes Miriam with leprosy. Why? Consider this possibility. In God's anger at Miriam, Moses' sister, God says in effect, "You like being light-skinned Miriam? I'll make you light-skinned." So we read, "When the cloud removed from over the tent, behold, Miriam was leprous, like snow" (Num. 12:10)."[171]

"The examples of Rahab and Ruth help us understand how God views the issue of marriage between those who are from different people groups but trust in the true God. Rahab was a Canaanite. These Canaanites had an ungodly culture, and were descendants of Canaan, the son of Ham. Remember, Canaan was cursed because of his obvious rebellious nature. Sadly, many Christians state that Ham was cursed—but this is not true. Some have even said that this (non-existent) curse of Ham resulted in the black 'races.' This is absurd and is the type of false teaching that has reinforced and justified prejudices against people with dark skin. In the genealogy in <u>Matthew 1</u>, it is traditionally understood that the same Rahab is listed here as being in the line leading to Christ. Thus Rahab, a descendant of Ham, must have married an Israelite (descended from Shem).

Since this was clearly a union approved by God, it underlines the fact that the particular 'people group' she came from was irrelevant—what mattered was that she trusted in the true God of the Israelites. The same can be said of Ruth, who as a Moabitess, also married an Israelite, and is also listed in the genealogy in Matthew 1 that leads to Christ. Prior to her marriage, she had expressed faith in the true God (Ruth 1:16). When Rahab and Ruth became children of God, there was no longer any barrier to Israelites marrying them, even though they were from different 'people groups.'"[172]

Salmon and Rahab

MATTHEW 1:5

Salmon begot Boaz by Rahab, Boaz begot Obed by Ruth, Obed begot Jesse,

Salmon is from the Semitic line of Ham's sons and she is from the Hammetic line of sons. This was a multiracial marriage. Next, notice: Boaz begot Obed by Ruth.

Boaz and Ruth

They were a multiracial couple. She was a Moabite and he was an Israelite.

David and Bathsheba

Bathsheba was a Cushite or from that region of Cush (modern day Ethiopia). The Cush ites were dark skinned people, and their skin color is often depicted in Ancient Egyptian Murals. Hays says "the Cushites were clearly black African people with negroid features."[173] It is safe to say that Bathsheba was a black, dark skinned woman. We also know the queen of Sheba was black. In Genesis 10:7 Sheba is listed as in Ham's family. That means that Solomon had to be a man of color. Some may ask; what about the children of multiracial couples? The interracial children are absolutely beautiful, and today they no longer face much racism from the next generation. Do you feel bad for President Obama, or Tiger Woods who are both multicultural?

In a recent article Fox News reported that "multiracial Americans are the fastest growing demographic group. Interracial marriages increased threefold to 4.3 million since 2000, when Alabama became the last state to lift its unenforceable ban on interracial marriages." The Supreme Court barred race-based restrictions on marriage in 1967. About 1 in 13 marriages are mixed race, with the most prevalent being white-Hispanic, white-American Indian and white-Asian. Multiracial unions have been happening for a very long time, but we are only now really coming to terms with saying it's OK," said Carolyn Liebler, a sociology professor at the University of Minnesota who specializes in family, race and ethnicity. "I don't think we've nearly tapped the potential. Millions are yet to come out."[174]

According to the New York Times, they found that 40 percent of Americans have dated someone of another race. The U.S. census revealed that, among native born, married, Americans ages 25-34 years old, over two-fifths of Hispanics and one-half of Asians had spouses who belonged to a different ethnic or racial group. The number of black-white couples alone tripled between the years of 1970 and 1991, and continues to grow. "When Christians legalistically impose non-biblical ideas such as no "interracial" marriage, they are helping to perpetuate prejudices that have often arisen from evolutionary influences. If we are really honest, in countries like America, the main reason some Christians forbid "interracial" marriage is not scriptural. They forbid "interracial marriage" because of preconceived prejudices. Besides, there has been so much mixing of people groups over the years that it would be impossible for many human beings today to trace their lineage back to know for certain from which group they are descended![175]

After reading this book, I encourage you to carefully consider the endnotes. They contain further studies, facts not found in the main body of the text, great commentator's concepts, ideas, illustrations and quotes.

For additional study material, please visit:
www.theblendedchurch.com
www.DehnerMaurer.com

ENDNOTES

[1] Boyd, David. You Don't Have To Cross The Ocean To Reach The World. Grand Rapids: Chosen, 2008. 102.

[2] Ibid, 102.

[3] George Yancey, *One Body One Spirit: Principles of Successful Multiracial Churches,* Downers Grove: Inter Varsity Press. 49.

[4] North American Mission Board of the Southern Baptist Convention (NAMB), *A Guide for Planting Multicultural Churches* (Alpharetta, GA: NAMB, 1999), 6.

[5] NAMB, 6.

[6] Mike Bergman, "Census Bureau Projects Tripling Of Hispanic And Asian Populations In 50 Years; Non-hispanic Whites May Drop To Half Of Total Population. " Http://www.census.gov, http://www.census.gov/Press-Release/www/releases/archives/population/001720.html. (accessed May 9,2009).

[7] NAMB.

[8] Robert B. Kruschwitz, "Introduction" in *Immigration: Christian Reflection* (Waco, TX: Baylor University, 2008), 8.

[9] Ibid,8.

10   Charles R. Foster, *Embracing Diversity: Leadership in Multicultural Congregations* (Herndon Virginia: Alban Institute Publication, 1997), 50.

11   Tony Campolo, *The Church Enslaved: A Spirituality Of Racial Reconciliation* (Minneapolis, Minnesota: Augsburg Fortress, 2005), 11.

12   James Cone, *Risks Of Faith: The Emergence of Black Theology Of Liberation* (Boston, Ma: Beacon Press, 2000.

13   Friedrich Otto Hertz. Quoted in *Draper's Book of Quotations for the Christian World,* ed. Edythe Draper (Wheaton: Tyndale House Publishers, Inc., 1992).

14   F. F. Bruce, *The New International Commentary On The New Testament: The Book Of Acts* (Grand Rapids: WM.B.Eerdmans, 1954), 358.

15   George, T. (2001, c1994). Vol. 30: Galatians (electronic ed.). Logos Library System; The New American Commentary (284). Nashville: Broadman & Holman Publishers. FIX

16   Hendriksen, W., & Kistemaker, S. J. (1953-2001). *New Testament Commentary :Exposition of Galatians. Vol. 8: Accompanying biblical text is author's translation. New Testament Commentary,* Grand Rapids: Baker Book House, 150.

17   A. Charles Ware, *Prejudice and the People Of God* (Indianapolis: Baptist Bible College, 1998), 86.

18   Walvoord, J. F., Zuck, R. B., & Dallas Theological Seminary. (1983-c1985). *The Bible Knowledge Commentary : An exposition of the scriptures* (2:387). Wheaton, IL: Victor Books.

[19] Easton, M. (1996, c1897). Easton's Bible Dictionary. Oak Harbor, WA: Logos Research Systems, Inc.

[20] Kistemaker, S. J., & Hendriksen, W. (1953-2001). *Vol. 17: New Testament commentary : Exposition of the Acts of the Apostles.* Accompanying biblical text is author's translation. New Testament Commentary (423). Grand Rapids: Baker Book House.

[21] My house shall be called a house of prayer for all the nations. St. Mark, writing for Gentiles, assures them that the God of the Jews is the God of all the nations; and that the court of the Gentiles, which was then so profaned, was a constituent part of his house of prayer. The Pulpit Commentary: St. Mark Vol. II. 2004 (H. D. M. Spence-Jones, Ed.) (122). Bellingham, WA: Logos Research Systems, Inc.

[22] Kistemaker, S. J., & Hendriksen, W. (1953-2001). *Vol. 17: New Testament commentary : Exposition of the Acts of the Apostles. Accompanying biblical text is author's translation. New Testament Commentary (376).* Grand Rapids: Baker Book House.

[23] Lev 11:1–47 presents a special diet for special people. After the events of 8–10, the recitation of laws continues with a list of permitted and forbidden foods—designated here and elsewhere in Scripture as "clean" and "unclean" animals. The Israelites could eat any animal with cloven hooves that chewed its cud, or any fish that had fins and scales. 20 birds were listed that could not be eaten. If someone touched an unclean animal, he was to wash his clothes and quarantine himself for 24 hours. (see exposition on Deut. 14:3–21) These regulations were

given to keep the Israelites clean. God was holy, and he wanted his people to be holy. While the dietary laws are no longer in force (Acts 10:9–16; Mark 7:19), God still wants his people to be holy (see 1 Pet. 1:16, which quotes 11:44). Willmington, H. L. (1997). Willmington's Bible handbook (68). Wheaton, Ill.: Tyndale House Publishers.

[24] Kistemaker, S. J., & Hendriksen, W. (1953-2001). *Vol. 17: New Testament commentary : Exposition of the Acts of the Apostles. Accompanying biblical text is author's translation. New Testament Commentary* (378). Grand Rapids: Baker Book House.

[25] Saying ... . understand is an admission that this is really new for him, and that only now, at long last, was he beginning to understand that the church was to include men from every nation. The truth of Jesus' words "I have other sheep, which are not of this fold" (John 10:16) was dawning. The meaning of the vision was clear. MacArthur, J. (1994, c1996). Acts (299). Chicago: Moody Press.

[26] Gaertner, D. (1993). *Acts. The College Press NIV commentary* (Ac 10:43). Joplin, Mo.: College Press.

[27] The features of this lovable man stand out in bold relief. In Acts 4 we see his magnificent generosity. In Acts 14 we see his impressive personality. In Acts 11 we see his innate goodness, and his notable Ministry. However in Acts 15 we see his lamentable contention. Herbert Lockyer, *All The Men Of The Bible* (Grand Rapids Michigan: Zondervan Publishing House 1958) 67-68.

28 MacArthur, J. J. (1997, c1997). *The MacArthur Study Bible* (electronic ed.) (Ga 2:11). Nashville: Word Pub.

29 Wiersbe, W. W. (1996, c1989). *The Bible exposition commentary.* "An exposition of the New Testament comprising the entire 'BE' series"—Jkt. (Ga 2:11). Wheaton, Il., Victor Books.

30 Ken Ham, *One Blood,* 58-59.

31 Cottrell, J. (1996-c1998). Romans : Volume 2. College Press NIV Commentary (Ro 10:12). Joplin, Mo.: College Press Pub. Co

32 MacArthur, J. J. (1997, c1997). *The MacArthur Study Bible* (electronic ed.) (Jas 2:1). Nashville: Word Pub.

33 Richardson, K. A. (2001, c1997). *Vol. 36: James* (electronic ed.). Logos Library System; The New American Commentary (108). Nashville: Broadman & Holman Publishers.

34 Loh, I., & Hatton, H. (1997). *A handbook on the Letter from James.* UBS handbook series (74). New York: United Bible Societies.

35 Davis, C. A. (2000). Revelation. The College Press NIV commentary (195). Joplin, Mo.: College Press Pub.

36 Kistemaker, S. J., & Hendriksen, W. (1953-2001). Vol. 20: New Testament commentary : Exposition of the Book of Revelation. Accompanying biblical text is author's translation. New Testament Commentary (253). Grand Rapids: Baker Book House.

37 The saints are dressed in white, which is a fulfillment of Jesus' promise to the church in Sardis that the faithful ones will be dressed in white (3:4, 5). The color white signifies holiness.

Furthermore, the souls under the altar were given white garments (6:11; see also 3:18; 4:4; 7:13). Here is a scene of heaven at the throne of God and the Lamb. The saints are dressed in white, which is a fulfillment of Jesus' promise to the church in Sardis that the faithful ones will be dressed in white (3:4, 5). The color white signifies holiness. In addition, the souls under the altar were given white garments (6:11; see also 3:18; 4:4; 7:13). Here is a scene of heaven at the throne of God and the Lamb. Kistemaker, S. J., & Hendriksen, W. (1953-2001). Vol. 20: New Testament commentary: Exposition of the Book of Revelation. Accompanying biblical text is author's translation. New Testament Commentary (254). Grand Rapids: Baker Book House.

38 2 Corinthians 5:17- Therefore, if anyone is in Christ, he is a new creation; old things have passed away; behold, all things have become new.

39 palms in ... hands—the antitype to Christ's entry into Jerusalem amidst the palm-bearing multitude. This shall be just when He is about to come visibly and take possession of His kingdom. The palm branch is the symbol of joy and triumph. It was used at the feast of tabernacles, on the fifteenth day of the seventh month, when they kept the feast to God in thanksgiving for the in gathered fruits. Jamieson, R., Fausset, A. R., Fausset, A. R., Brown, D., & Brown, D. (1997). A commentary, critical and explanatory, on the Old and New Testaments. On spine: Critical and explanatory commentary. (Re 7:9). Oak Harbor, WA: Logos Research Systems, Inc.

[40] John 12:12-13. The next day a great multitude that had come to the feast, when they heard that Jesus was coming to Jerusalem, took branches of palm trees and went out to meet Him, and cried out: " Hosanna! ' Blessed is He who comes in the name of the LORD! The King of Israel!"

[41] Kistemaker, S. J., & Hendriksen, W. (1953-2001). Vol. 20: New Testament commentary : Exposition of the Book of Revelation. Accompanying biblical text is author's translation. New Testament Commentary (211). Grand Rapids: Baker Book House.

[42] *The Pulpit Commentary: Revelation.* 2004 (H. D. M. Spence-Jones, Ed.) (166). Bellingham, WA: Logos Research Systems, Inc.

[43] J. Daniel Hays, *From Every People and Nation: A Biblical Theology Of Race, New Studies In Biblical Theology, ed. D. A. Carson, vol. 14* (Downers Grove, Illinois: InterVarsity Press, 2003), 199.

[44] Wanda A. Turner. *Celebrate Change: Embracing Life's Changing Seasons* (Shippensburg, Pennsylvania: Treasure House, 2001.)

[45] Galatians 6:9 And let us not grow weary while doing good, for in due season we shall reap if we do not lose heart.

[46] Luke 14:7-11 So He told a parable to those who were invited, when He noted how they chose the best places, saying to them: "When you are invited by anyone to a wedding feast, do not sit down in the best place, lest one more honorable than you be invited by him; and he who invited you and him come and say to you, 'Give place to this man,' and then you begin with shame to take the lowest place. 10 But when you are invited,

go and sit down in the lowest place, so that when he who invited you comes he may say to you, 'Friend, go up higher.' Then you will have glory in the presence of those who sit at the table with you. For whoever exalts himself will be humbled, and he who humbles himself will be exalted."

[47] SAMARITANS- Schismatic group from the Jews. The group resided north of Judea and south of Galilee in hostile tension with its Jewish neighbors. Jesus' attitude toward this despised group radically contrasted with contemporary sentiment. Both Jews and the Samaritans excluded the other from their respective cultic centers, the Jerusalem temple and the Samaritan temple on Mt Gerizim. The Samaritans, for example, were forbidden access to the inner courts of the temple, and any offering they might give was considered as if it were from a Gentile. Thus, although probably more accurately defined as "schismatics," it appears Samaritans were in practice treated as Gentiles. All marriage between the groups was therefore, forbidden, and social relations were greatly restricted (Jn 4:9). With such proscribed separation, it is not surprising that any interaction between the two groups was strained. Samaritan was a term of contempt on the lips of Jews (8:48), and among some scribes it possibly would not even be uttered (see the apparent circumlocution in Lk 10:37). The disciples' reaction to the Samaritan refusal of lodging (9:51–55) is a good example of the animosity felt by Jews for Samaritans at the time. Elwell, W. A., & Comfort, P. W. (2001). Tyndale Bible dictionary. Tyndale reference library (1154). Wheaton, Ill.: Tyndale House Publishers.

[48] SHECHEM. 1. Called also SICHEM and SYCHEM, a district in the central part of the land of Canaan. Abraham dwells in, Gen. 12:6. Jacob buys a piece of ground in, and erects an altar, Gen. 33:18–20. The flocks and herds of Jacob kept in, Gen. 37:12–14. Joseph buried in, Josh. 24:32. Jacob buried in, Acts 7:16, with Gen. 50:13. 2. Called also SYCHAR, a city of refuge in Mount Ephraim, Josh. 20:7; 21:21; Judg. 21:19. Joshua assembled the tribes of Israel at, with all their elders, chiefs, and judges, and presented them before the Lord, Josh. 24:1–28. Joshua buried at, Josh. 24:30–32. Abimelech made king at, Judg. 8:31; 9. Rehoboam crowned at, 1 Kin. 12:1. Destroyed by Abimelech, Judg. 9:45; rebuilt by Jeroboam, 1 Kin. 12:25. Men of, slain by Ishmael, Jer. 41:5. Jesus visits; disciples made in, John 4:1–42. 3. Son of Hamor; seduces Jacob's daughter; slain by Jacob's sons, Gen. 33:19; 34; Josh. 24:32; Judg. 9:28. Called SYCHEM, Acts 7:16. 4. Ancestor of the Shechemites, Num. 26:31; Josh. 17:2. 5. Son of Shemidah, 1 Chr. 7:19. Swanson, J., & Nave, O. (1994). *New Nave's Topical Bible*. Oak Harbor: Logos Research Systems.

[49] Jesus was different. He spoke to her as God spoke to Hagar and as Abraham's servant spoke to Rebekah in ancient times. This woman was really being treated like a person. Jesus even wanted a drink from her (John 4:7). What would the disciples have said if they had been around? Fortunately, they were conveniently out of the way looking for kosher food in Samaria (4:8). The woman did not know what to make of such an overture. Jesus did not fit the stereotype of kosher-concerned Jewish men. Her first response, therefore, was to question him about

his unexpected freedom in conversation (4:9). Borchert, G. L. (2001, c1996). Vol. 25A: John 1-11 (electronic ed.). Logos Library System; The New American Commentary (202). Nashville: Broadman & Holman Publishers.

[50] Christian History Institute, "Birmingham Blast: Why Children?," *Christian History Institute,* April 2007, 2007, http://chi.gospelcom.net/DAILYF/2001/09/daily-09-15-2001.shtml/ (accessed Sept 1, 2007).

[51] Library of Congress, "African American Odyssey: A Quest For Full Citizenship." *Civil Rights Era,* Oct 1, 2002, http://memory.loc.gov/ammem/aaohtml/exhibit/aopart9b.html/ (accessed Sept 7, 2007).

[52] In v. 10, Jesus tells her that she is ignorant of two things: the gift of God (salvation) and the identity of the Savior in her presence. Jesus speaks of living water—water of life—but she takes this to mean literal water. How typical of the sinner, confusing the physical and the spiritual! Nicodemus thought Christ spoke of physical birth (3:4), and even the disciples thought He spoke of literal food later on (4:31–34). Jesus points out to her that the things of the world do not satisfy, and men without Christ will always "thirst again." The parable in Luke 16:19–31 makes this so clear; the rich man who thirsted after physical pleasures in this life thirsted again when he found himself in Hades. Jesus promises that the water of life will spring up within the heart and keep us constantly refreshed and satisfied: and the woman, still confused, asked for that water. It was a shallow emotional response. Wiersbe,

W. W. (1997, c1992). Wiersbe's expository outlines on the New Testament (220). Wheaton, Il., Victor Books.

[53] Is Door Knocking In Personal Work Dead? We know door knocking worked in Jesus' day because his disciples came back all excited about their success, Luke 10:17-20. The church continued to experience success in door knocking, Acts 5:42. The church multiplied in number, 6:7. Why did door knocking work so well then? Those Christians who approached the lost in the early church, had a message that moved the lost to want eternal life. Their approach was not an invitation to a church meeting or to take a course by mail with the promise that no one would call on them. They taught Christ and him crucified, 1 Corinthians 2:2. The early church was also interested in helping physically, Galatians 6:10. Jesus' example of Matthew 14:14-21 had taught the disciples to be concerned for the physical & spiritual needs of the lost. In Door Knocking Today. The week that I wrote this article a member of our congregation came to me and said that he had been contacted by 3 different groups in one week through door knocking. One of those groups is growing very rapidly through door knocking and studies. I recently returned from a door knocking training session in Morrilton, AR. There I knocked 27 doors of which 18 were home. Thirteen of the eighteen allowed me to present the gospel to them. Yes, door knocking will work! It will if we will. Bob Danklefsen, "Is Door Knocking In Personal Work Dead?," *www.bible.ca.* http://www.bible.ca/evangelism/e-door-knocking.htm. (accessed August 14, 2007).

54 GERIZIM, MOUNT -Mountain (modern Jebel et-Tor) from which the blessings were to be pronounced, just as the cursings were to come from Mt Ebal (Dt 11:29). The two mountains designated by God were opposite each other, and the setting was a memorable one with six tribes positioned on Mt Gerizim and six on Mt Ebal, the Levites standing in the valley between—reciting the blessings and the cursings (Dt 27:11–28:68; Jos 8:33–35). The mountain is near Shechem, about 10 miles (16.1 kilometers) southeast of the city of Samaria, and it is referred to by the woman of Samaria in John 4:20–23 as the mountain where "our fathers worshiped." Abraham, indeed, had built an altar in this area (Gn 12:6–7; 33:18–20), and it had been the revered site for Samaritan worship for centuries. Jesus responds to the woman by pointing out that the physical locality of worship (whether Gerizim or Jerusalem) is not important—the spirtual reality is. One must worship in spirit and in truth. Elwell, W. A., & Comfort, P. W. (2001). Tyndale Bible dictionary. Tyndale reference library (526). Wheaton, Ill.: Tyndale House Publishers

55 Mary C. Turck, "Kids Fight For Civil Rights," *Rethinking Schools Online,* Spring 2004, 2000, http://www.rethinkingschools.org/archive/18_03/kids183.shtml/ (accessed August 13, 2007).

56 Martin Luther King Jr., "I Have a Dream Speech," U S Constitution Online, July 30, 2007, 1963, http://www.usconstitution.net/dream.html, / (accessed August 12, 2007).

57 Jesus' intuitive knowledge of the woman's personal life and his ability to answer a difficult question about the place of

worship led the woman to think of him as a possible Samaritan Messiah, who, in her Samaritan thinking would be a prophet-teacher, called Taheb (probably meaning "the one who restores" or perhaps "the one who returns"). This Messiah would teach the people and explain all things. Jews did not seemingly think primarily of their Messiah as a teacher, unless it was as a teacher of the Gentiles. The woman said that when Messiah came, he would explain everything to us. This statement is both revealing and concealing: it reveals that a modicum of belief in Jesus is in the woman, but it conceals her doubts and the immaturity of her faith. It does, however, enable Jesus to reveal himself to her in verse 26, "I, the one speaking to you, am he (the Messiah). Bryant, B. H., & Krause, M. S. (1998). John. The College Press NIV commentary (Jn 4:25). Joplin, Mo.: College Press Pub. Co.

[58] 1 John 2:9-11, James 2:8-9.

[59] I have food. Just like the Samaritan woman's misunderstanding of Jesus words regarding literal water (v. 15), Jesus' own disciples thought only of literal food. John commonly used such misunderstanding to advance the argument of his gospel (e.g., 2:20; 3:3). MacArthur, J. J. (1997, c1997). The MacArthur Study Bible (electronic ed.) (Jn 4:32). Nashville: Word Pub.

Surely, no one has brought him food? It is hard for them to imagine that in the land of the Samaritans anyone could have brought food to Jesus! Hendriksen, W., & Kistemaker, S. J. (1953-2001). Vol. 1-2: New Testament commentary Exposition of the Gospel According to John. Accompanying

biblical text is author's translation. New Testament
Commentary (1:172). Grand Rapids: Baker Book House.

[60] Emmanuel Johnson, *I'm Not Black, You're Not White*
(Shippensburg, Pennsylvania: Destiny Image Publishers, 1990),
21.

[61] Kelly Varner, *The Three Prejudices*, 128.

[62] Ibid, 128.

[63] Scott A. Bradley, *The Black Man: Cursed Or Blessed*
(Bellwood, Illinois: Rivers Of Life Ministry, 1993), 5.

[64] George Yancy, Curtiss Paul DeYoung, Michael Emmerson,
Karen Chai Kim, Tony Campolo, David Anderson, and
Manuel Ortiz.

[65] One experiment that may confirm my thesis was the actions of
Bishop Fred A. Caldwell. Bishop Caldwell pastors a large
African American congregation in Shreveport, Louisiana. He
wanted to build a multicultural church so he began to pay
non-blacks five dollars an hour to sit through Sunday morning
services and ten dollars an hour to attend the churches
Thursday night service. This experiment was soon picked up
by the local Shreveport newspaper and in papers across the
United States including the USA Today. Reports after one year
were that thousands of dollars were spent but the church was
right back where it started as being predominantly African-
American. Michael O. Emerson. *People Of The Dream*
(Princeton New Jersey: Princeton University Press, 2006) 9-10.

[66] Laurene Beth Bowers, *Becoming A Multicultural Church*, 97-98.

[67] Christ-ucc.org/Anti-Racism/CACResoloution.doc. (accessed July, 2008).

[68] Being Church And Overcoming Racism: It's Time For Transformative Justice. World Council of Churches Central Committee. Http://www2.wcc- Coe.org/ccdocuments.nsf/index/plen-4-en.html," / (accessed August 2009).

[69] David Tame, *The Secret Power Of Music* (New York, New York: Destiny Books, 1984), 34.

[70] Michael O. Emerson, Curtiss Paul DeYoung et al., *United By Faith: The Multicultural Congregation As An Answer To The Problem Of Race*, 176.

[71] Julie Blim and Kristi Watts, "Israel Houghton: An Intimate Portrait of Worship," CBN Music. Com. http://www.cbn.com/cbnmusic/Interviews/700club_IsraelHoughton_041205.aspx. / (accessed July 5, 2009).

[72] A Short Catechism on the Tabernacle of David by Bob Johnson. http://www.tabernacle-of-david.com/catechism.html. (Accessed April, 2007).

[73] Damian O. Emetuche, "Issues In Planting A Multicultural Church," *Globalmissionary.org*, http://www.globalmissiology.org/portugues/docs_pdf/featured/emetuche_issues_planting_multicultural_church_2_2009.pdf. (accessed August, 2009).

[74] Thus, when St. John had a vision of the New Jerusalem, he was ordered to write, Rev. 21:5. He must write it, that he might imprint it on his own mind, and make it more clear to himself, but especially that it might be notified to those in distant places and transmitted to those in future ages. What is

handed down by tradition is easily mistaken and liable to corruption; but what is written is reduced to a certainty, and preserved safe and pure. We have reason to bless God for written visions, that God has written to us the great things of his prophets as well as of his law. He must write the vision, and make it plain upon tables, must write it legibly, in large characters, so that he who runs may read it, that those who will not allow themselves leisure to read it deliberately may not avoid a cursory view of it. Probably, the prophets were wont to write some of the most remarkable of their predictions in tables, and to hang them up in the temple, Isaiah 8:1. Now the prophet is told to write this very plain. Note, Those who are employed in preaching the word of God should study plainness as much as may be, so as to make themselves intelligible to the meanest capacities. The things of our everlasting peace, which God has written to us, are made plain, they are all plain to him that understands (Prov. 8:9), and they are published with authority; God himself has prefixed his imprimatur to them; he has said, Make them plain. Henry, M. (1996, c1991). Matthew Henry's commentary on the whole Bible : Complete and unabridged in one volume (Hab 2:1). Peabody: Hendrickson.

[75] **John 12:24** Most assuredly, I say to you, unless a grain of wheat falls into the ground and dies, it remains alone; but if it dies, it produces much grain.

[76] http://www.fasttrackteaching.com/termsmodern.html. (Accessed Sept, 2008)

[77] Charles R. Foster, *Embracing Diversity,* 3.

[78] Ibid, 3.

[79] George Yancey, *One Body One Spirit*, 130-131.

[80] David A. Anderson, *Multicultural Ministry: Finding Your Churches Unique Rhythm* (Grand Rapids Michigan: Zondervan Press, 2004), 37.

[81] Michael O. Emerson, Curtiss Paul DeYoung et al., *United By Faith: The Multicultural Congregation As An Answer To The Problem Of Race*, 178

[82] Scott Thumma and Dave Travis, *Beyond Megachurch Myths* (San Francisco: Jossey Bass, 2007), 138.

[83] Being Church And Overcoming Racism: It's Time For Transformative Justice. World Council Of Churches Central Committee. Http://www2.wcc- Coe.org/ccdocuments.nsf/index/plen-4-en.html," / (accessed August 2009).

[84] *P.B.S,* http://www.pbs.org/wgbh/pages/frontline/shows/divided/etc/synopsis.html," www.pbs.com/ (accessed January, 2009).

[85] Jack Hayford, *Out Racing the World: An Appeal to TransEthnicity* (Van Nuys: Living Way Ministries, 1994), 5.

[86] Liston Pope, *The Kingdom Beyond Castle* (New York, New York: Frenchship Press, 1957), 105.

[87] Joe Fagan and Eileen O'Brien, *White Men On Race: Power, Privilege, And The Shaping Of Cultural Consciousness* (Boston, Massachusetts: Beacon Press, 2003), 98.

[88] Manuel Ortiz, *One New People: Models for Developing A Multiethnic Church* (Downers Grove, Illinois: Inter Varsity Press, 1996), 26.

89 Jack Hayford, *Out Racing the World: An Appeal to Trans Ethnicity,* 5.

90 Laurene Beth Bowers, *Becoming A Multicultural Church* (Cleveland, Ohio: The Pilgrim Press, 2006), 27.

91 Anthony B. Pinn, *The Black Church in the Post-Civil Rights Era* (Maryknoll, New York: Orbis Books, 2002), 135.

92 Raymond Blanks, *Ending Racism in the Church* (Cleveland: United Church Press, 1998), 103.

93 George Yancey, *One Body One Spirit: Principles of Successful Multiracial Churches.* (Downers Grove, Illinois: Inter Varsity Press, 2003) 113.

94 John 17:1-26.

95 Fagan and O'Brien, *White Men on Race,* 9.

96 Michael Moncur, "The Quotations Page," , http://www.quotationpage.com/quote/26032.html. (accessed July 20, 2009).

97 Laurene Beth Bowers, *Becoming A Multicultural Church,* 16.

98 Alonzo Johnson, *Ending Racism In The Church,* ed. Susan E. Davies and Sister Paul Teresa Hennessy (Cleveland, Ohio: United Church Press, 1998), 64.

99 Bernard T. Adeney, *Strange Virtues: Ethics in a Multicultural World* (Downers Grove, Illinois: InterVarsity Press, 1995), 16.

100 Leslie Newbigin, *Foolishness To The Greeks* (Grand Rapids Michigan: Erdmann's Publishing,), 3.

101 E.D. Hirsh, Jr., Joesph F. Kett, and James Trefil, *Dictionary Of Cultural Literacy 2nd edition* (Boston, Massachusetts: Houghton Mifflin, 1993), 415.

102 ABC News, *We're All The Same,* (September 10, 1998).

103 Ham, Ken. Ware Charles. *Darwin's Plantation: Evolution's Racist Roots.* Master Books, 2007. Chapter 5.

104 Ken Ham, Carl Weiland, and Don Batten, *One Blood: The Biblical Answer To Racism* (Green Forest, Arkansas: Master Books Inc, 1999), 53-55.

105 Ortiz, Manuel. *One New People: Models for Developing a Multiethnic Church.* (Downers Grove: InterVarsity Press, 1996), 93.

106 Michael O. Emerson, Curtiss Paul DeYoung, *United By Faith: The Multicultural Congregation As An Answer To The Problem Of Race* (New York, New York: Oxford University Press, 2003), 29, 155.

107 Kelly Varner, *The Three Prejudices: Gender, Race, Nation* (Shippensburg, Pennsylvania: Destiny Image Publishers, 1997), 26.

108 Steven Rhoads, *Where Nations Meet: The Church In A Multicultural World* (Downers Grove, Illinois: InterVarsity Press, 1998), 17.

109 Ken Davis, "Multicultural Church Planting Models," *The Journal of Ministry & Theology* (Spring 2003),115.

110 Tony Campolo, *The Church Enslaved: A Spirituality of Racial Reconciliation,* 11.

111 George Yancey, *One Body One Spirit: Principles Of Successful Multiracial Churches,* 18.

112 Frederick K.C. Price *Race Religion and Racism,* (Los Angeles, California: Faith One Publishing, 1999) 7.

[113] John Wallis, "White Church Black Church." *Next Wave.* http://www.next-wave.org/jul01/whiteblackchurch.htm. (accessed August 1, 2009).

[114] Curtiss Paul DeYoung, Michael O. Emerson, George Yancey, and Karen Chai Kim. *United By Faith: The Multicultural Congregation As An Answer To The Problem of Race.* New York: Oxford University Press, 2003

[115] Jonathan Wilson-Hartgrove, *Free To Be Bound: Church Behond the Color Line* (Colorado Springs: Navpress, 2008), 87.

[116] Emile Durkheim, *The Elementary Forms Of the Religious Life* (New York: Free Press, 1915).

[117] Jack Hayford, *Out Racing the World: An Appeal to TransEthnicity,* 15-16.

[118] Tony Campolo and Michael Battle, *The Church Enslaved: A Spirituality of Racial Reconciliation,* 74.

[119] Laurene Beth Bowers, *Becoming a Multicultural Church,* 17.

[120] Joe R. Feagin, Hernán Vera, and Pinar Batur, *White Racism: The Basics,* 2nd ed. (New York: Routledge, 2001), 187-189.

[121] Jennifer Hochschild, *Facing Up to the American Dream* (Princeton: Princeton University Press, 1995), 264.

[122] David A. Anderson, *Finding Your Church's Unique Rhythm: Multicultural Ministry,* 45-46.

[123] Jack W. Hayford, "Confessing What Separates Us," in *Ending Racism in the Church,* 17.

[124] **John 8:43-44** Why do you not understand My speech? Because you are not able to listen to My word. You are of your father

the devil, and the desires of your father you want to do. He was a murderer from the beginning, and does not stand in the truth, because there is no truth in him. When he speaks a lie, he speaks from his own resources, for he is a liar and the father of it.

[125] Joe Feagin & Eileen O'Brien, *White Men on Race: Power, Privilege, and the Shaping of Cultural Consciousness,* 14.

[126] Laurene Beth Bowers, *Becoming a Multicultural Church,* 29.

[127] Paul Kivel, *Uprooting Racism: How White People Can Work for Racial Justice,* 40.

[128] John Wallis, "White Church, Black Church," *Next-wave,* July, 2001, http://www.next-wave.org/jul01/whiteblackchurch.htm. (accessed June 24, 2009).

[129] Jack W. Hayford, "Confessing What Separates Us," in *Ending Racism in the Church,* 21.

[130] Cyrus Ingerson Scofield was born in 1843 and died in 1921. Scofield fought in the Confederate Army and was a lawyer before converting to Christianity in 1879. After working as a volunteer with the St. Louis YMCA in studying the Bible with a well-known minister, he was chosen to be a pastor in Dallas where he became fascinated with the Bible. According to J. William T. Young's, Scofield never learned the original tongues of the Bible, and he rejected higher criticism as leading to apostasy. He held the every word of the Bible- even as translated into English- was divinely inspired. His name in compiling the Scofield Bible was to aid his followers in finding what he considered biblical truths through his notes on various topics. The work he is best remembered for is the Scofield

reference Bible in 1909. Henry Warner Bowden, Dictionary of American Religious Biography, 2nd ed. Rev. and enl., s.v., "Scofield, Cyrus Ingerson" (Westport, Connecticut: Greenwood Press, 1993), 477

[131] Finis Jennings Dake was born in 1902 and died in 1987. He was ordained to the New Mexico- Texas District assemblies of God in 1927, pastored in the Dallas area and then became an evangelist in Oklahoma. In 1932, he became pastor of the Christian assembly in Zion, Illinois, where he established the Great Lakes Bible Institute, which later merged with Central Bible Institute. As a result of a controversy involving the violation of the federal Mann Act, which Dake's lawyer referred to as an unfortunate mistake, Dake's relationship with the Assemblies of God ended in 1937. Not allowing this to change his life's course, he remained Pentecostal, joined the church of God in Cleveland, Tennessee and eventually became independent. He authored popular tracks, books and pamphlets, but is best remembered for the Dake's Annotated Reference Bible. Finis Jennings Dake. ed., Dake's Annotated Reference Bible (Lawrenceville, Georgia: Dake Bible Sales., 1963, 1971) 159 [New Testament].

[132] Stanley M. Burgess and Gary B. McGee, *The Dictionary of Pentecostal and Charismatic Movements* (Grand Rapids Michigan: Zondervan Publishing House, 1988), 235.

[133] John F. Walvoord, *The Millennial Kingdom* (Grand Rapids: Zondervan Publishing House, 1959) p. 12 — quoted by Tim LaHaye, *Revelation –Illustrated and Made Plain* (Grand Rapids, MI: Zondervan Publishing House, 1973) 288.

[134] Cyrus Ingerson Scofield, *The Scofield Reference Bible* (New York, New York: Oxford University press, 1917 Revised), 16.

[135] *Mississippi Burning*, mis. Francis McDormand, 128 minutes. (Orion Pictures Corporation, 1989).

[136] William DeWhite McKissick, Sr, *Beyond Roots: In Search Of Blacks In The Bible*. (Wenonah, New Jersey: Renaissance Productions, 1990) 16-17.

[137] Luther Blackwell, *The Heritage Of The Black Believer*, (Shippensburg: Treasure House, 1993.) 50-55.

[138] Anthony T. Evans, *Are Blacks Spiritually Inferior To Whites*, (New Jersey: Renaissance Productions, 1992.) 15.

[139] Tee Garlington, *Ending Racism In The Church*, ed. Susan E. Davies and Sister Paul Theresa Hennessey, 77.

[140] Richard Herrnstein and Charles Murry, *The Bell Curve* (New York, New York: Free Press, 1994), 269-340.

[141] Steven Fraser, *The Bell Curve Wars*, ed. Steven Fraser (New York, New York: Basic Books, 1995), 3-4.

[142] Sharon Begley, "Three Is Not Enough," *Newsweek*, February 13, 1995, 67 .

[143] Eric C. Lincoln and Lawrence H. Mamiya, *The Black Church in the American Experience* (Durham: Duke University Press, 1990), 8.

[144] Craig Van Gelder, *The Essence of the Church: A Community Created by the Spirit* (Grand Rapids: Baker Books, 2000), 72.

[145] Laurie F. Maffly-Kipp, "The Church in the Southern Black Community," *Documenting The American South*, May, 2001,

http://docsouth.unc.edu/church/intro.html. (accessed April 10, 2009).

[146] Ibid

[147] Tony Campolo and Michael Battle, *The Church Enslaved: A Spirituality of Racial Reconciliation*, 59.

[148] Ibid, 60–63.

[149] Ibid, 64.

[150] Ibid, 67–68.

[151] Kim E. Gordon, "Why Are Most Blacks Always Late? (C.P. Time)," *Capital City Courier*, April, 2007, 7.

[152] Ibid, 10.

[153] Anthony Vader, "What You Can Learn From African-American Liturgy," *American Catholic Press*, October, 1996, http://www.americancatholicpress.org/Father_Vader_African_American_Liturgy.html. (accessed May 5, 2009).

[154] Tony Campolo and Michael Battle, *The Church Enslaved: A Spirituality of Racial Reconciliation*, 67–68.

[155] Michael O. Emerson, Curtiss Paul DeYoung et al., *United By Faith: The Multicultural Congregation As An Answer To The Problem Of Race*, 110.

[156] James Cone, *A Black Theology Of Liberation* (New York: Lippincott, 1970), 58-60.

[157] J. Deotis Roberts, *Liberation and Reconciliation: A Black Theology* (Philadelphia, Pennsylvania: Westminster Press, 1971), 83.

[158] Anthony B. Pinn, *The Black Church In The Post-Civil Rights Era*, 38.

[159] Ron Rhodes, *Black Theology, Black Power, And The Black Experience."* Part Two In A Three-part Series On Liberation Theology, accessed April 2009, http://home.earthlink.net/~ronrhodes/BlackTheology.html.

[160] Shem—The historian introduces him with marked distinction as "the father of Eber," the ancestor of the Hebrews. Jamieson, R., Fausset, A. R., Fausset, A. R., Brown, D., & Brown, D. (1997). A commentary, critical and explanatory, on the Old and New Testaments. On spine: Critical and explanatory commentary. (Ge 10:21). Oak Harbor, WA: Logos Research Systems, Inc.

[161] Tony Campolo, *The Church Enslaved: A Spirituality Of Racial Reconciliation,* 24.

[162] James H. Cone, *Martin and Malcolm and America: A Dream or a Nightmare* (Maryknoll, New York: Orbis Books, 1991) 151.

[163] Louis Abdul Farrakhan, original name Louis Eugene Walcott. Born May 11, 1933, Bronx, New York, N.Y. Leader (1978–2007) of the Nation of Islam, an African American movement that combined elements of Islam with black nationalism. http://www.biography.com/articles/Louis-Farrakhan-9291850, 1994-2008 Encyclopædia Britannica, Inc. Accessed January 2009.

[164] *Farrakhan: Charismatic Beacon or Cult Leader,* Videocassette, ctn. Glenn R. Plummer, 59 min. (Detroit Michigan: CTN TV Channel 26 Detroit, 1995).

165   Ken Ham, "Is Interracial Marriage Biblical," Answersingensis.org, June 1999, Http://www.answersingenesis.org/creation/v21/i3/ interracial.asp/ (accessed October 2008).

166   Gotquestions.org, *What Does The Bible Say About Interracial Marriages,"* http://www.gotquestions.org/interracial-marriage.html. (accessed June 2009).

167   Ken Ham, "Is Interracial Marriage Biblical," Answersingensis.org.

168   We would argue, rather, that "he," the subject of verse 15a, means God and that "one," the object, means the "one flesh" of Genesis 2:24. Verse 15a could then be paraphrased and explained: Why did God make Adam and Eve only one flesh, when He might have given Adam many wives, for God certainly had more than enough of the Spirit, or creative power, to furnish many partners? However, because God was seeking a godly offspring, He restricted man and woman to a single bonding, for He knew that a plurality of mates for either partner was not conducive to raising children to the glory of God. Kaiser, W. C., & Ogilvie, L. J. (1992). Vol. 23: The Preacher's Commentary Series, Volume 23 : Micah, Nahum, Habakkuk, Zephaniah, Haggai, Zechariah, Malachi. Formerly The Communicator's Commentary. The Preacher's Commentary series (488). Nashville, Tennessee: Thomas Nelson Inc.

169   Moses had brought into his tent a Cushite woman, one of the dark-skinned race which seemed even lower in the religious scale than the Egyptians themselves. Such an alliance might easily seem to Miriam nothing better than an act of apostasy which would justify any possible opposition. The Pulpit

Commentary: Numbers. 2004 (H. D. M. Spence-Jones, Ed.) (130). Bellingham, WA: Logos Research Systems, Inc.

An Ethiopian woman—Hebrew, "a Cushite woman"—Arabia was usually called in Scripture the land of Cush, its inhabitants being descendants of that son of Ham (see on Ex 2:15) and being accounted generally a vile and contemptible race (see on Am 9:7). Jamieson, R., Fausset, A. R., Fausset, A. R., Brown, D., & Brown, D. (1997). A commentary, critical and explanatory, on the Old and New Testaments. On spine: Critical and explanatory commentary. (Nu 12:1). Oak Harbor, WA: Logos Research Systems, Inc.

Miriam's questioning the Cushite origin of Moses' wife was but a smokescreen for her central concern, but the ethnic issue was a timely one for the Israelites. The rabble of mixed origins had instigated a rebellion that led to considerable loss of life for the community. Miriam may have been suggesting that a little ethnic cleansing might be beneficial to the survival of the Israelites. The term Cushite refers to distinguishable physiological features that would have made her distinctive, in which case the deeply tanned Midianites from northwest Arabia could be implied by the text. Whichever was intended in the case raised by Miriam, the questioning of Moses' exclusive right as Israel's leader was at the heart of the issue, though based on a questioning of his wife's ethnicity. Cole, R. D. (2001, c2000). Vol. 3B: Numbers (electronic ed.). Logos Library System; The New American Commentary (200) Nashville: Broadman & Holman Publishers.

[170] J. Daniel Hays, *From Every People and Nation* (Downers Grove: Inter Varsity Press, 2003), 71.

[171] John Piper, "Did Moses Marry A Black Woman," *Nine Marks,* 2008, 2009, http://www.9marks.org/partner/Article_Display_Page/0,,PTID314526%7CCHID598014%7CCIID2359816,00.html. (accessed July 31,09).

[172] Ken Ham, "Is Interracial Marriage Biblical," Answersingensis.org, June 1999, http://www.answersingenesis.org/creation/v21/i3/interracial.asp/ (accessed October 2008).

[173] J. Daniel Hays, *From Every People and Nation* (Downers Grove: Inter Varsity Press, 2003), 36.

[174] Associated Press, "Multi Racial Americans Fastest Growing Demographic Group," Fox News, May 28, 2009, http://www.foxnews.com/story/0,2933,522684,00.html. (accessed July 2009).

[175] Charles Ware, Ken Ham, *Darwin's Plantation: Evolution's Racist Roots.* Master Books, 2007), Chapter 6.